Painting by Dewitt Pyeatt, 1945

WINGED HISTORY

The Life and Times of
Kenneth L. Chastain, Aviator

UPDATED EDITION

By Kenneth L. Chastain, Jr.

Turner Publishing Company
www.turnerpublishing.com

Winged History: The Life and Times of Kenneth L. Chastain, Aviator,
      Updated Edition
Copyright © 2003 Kenneth L. Chastain, Jr.

Cover design: Mike Penticost
Book design: Mike Penticost

Library of Congress Cataloging-in-Publication Data

ISBN 978-1-56311-931-6 (hc)
ISBN 978-1-62045-828-0 (pbk)

In memory of my father, who showed me the meaning of passion, and my mother, who brought me into this world and taught me love during her short stay here on Earth.

Spears Odyssey

Flying Blind

Fly Me to Brazil

CONTENTS

PROLOGUE

In 1903, two brothers named Wright flew a small, fragile, powered aircraft for the first time in history. At the time, the general populace paid little heed to this momentous event. How were they to know the mammoth effect this single occurrence would have on people's lives? One life that was affected was that of my father, Kenneth Lee Chastain.

Until Charles Lindbergh's solo transatlantic flight, most Americans thought anyone flying the primitive aircraft of the time was crazy, but after Lindbergh's 1927 flight, pilots became heroes. In that innocent era of American history, people believed Lindbergh had been sent by God to perform this mighty feat. The public adulation of him was unique to the time and changed the country's perception of flying forever. After Lindbergh, suddenly people wanted either to fly or to invest in aviation.

My father was just beginning high school in the period after the Lindbergh phenomenon and was caught up in the excitement. His initial foray into the field was building model airplanes, a hobby he would enjoy throughout his life. He also began working part-time under supervision on aircraft and engines at an airport near his home.

As I have grown older, I have come to the realization that what I know, that is, my "common knowledge" of the world around me, is rapidly disappearing. The knowledge that a society shares in common changes over time. In many respects, this is a good thing. That is how new ideas are born and how innovative advancements are made. But there is a downside to this shift in the universal, everyday knowledge base of a people. That is, sadly, the fact that many good and precious experiences, awareness, and memories become forever lost.

I feel this loss personally and deeply. As I observe this shift in the societal lore of my lifetime, I feel as though my own personal history is becoming more and more irrelevant. The things that have brought me joy throughout my life and the memories that to this day warm my spirit, will one day be completely forgotten.

I observed this firsthand in the case of my father. In the last years of his life I went through his pictures with him, writing down each story that each photograph brought surging forth. I also documented his history, year by year, mixing the information I got from the photograph stories with data from his personal records, and from his answers to my direct questions. However, after he was gone and I tried to put all of that information together in a comprehensive way, I found gaping holes, pieces of his history I had failed to capture in time. There are parts of my father's story that are now gone forever.

It was with this in mind that I wrote this story of my father's life. By telling his story and how it fit into the history of his time, I hoped to establish a knowledge and pride in his life experiences. My goal was to write down what I learned of his history before it was lost forever. This is also meant to be a celebration of his life, for he was one of a generation of Americans born in the early part of the twentieth century who were extraordinary and very special people.

My father's generation emerged into a rural land where both communications and travel were very slow-paced. A significant portion of the American population at the time didn't even have electricity in their homes. Born into modest beginnings, his generation endured the Great Depression, took part in the most destructive war in history, and became a part of the complete makeover of the United States.

These people learned to share and help one another because they grew up with modest means. They outlasted the Depression only to be thrown into the Second World War. With a patriotic spirit, this generation put their lives aside to fight to keep their country free from tyranny. After the war, they suppressed the horrors and hardships they experienced and stepped up to the task of building the modern society we have today. Tom Brokaw, in his book of the same name, called it "the greatest generation"—and it truly was.

Kenneth Lee Chastain, Aviator

Chapter 1
The Early Years

A birth, a life, a destiny
Shed shackles of the poor
And sprang from simple roots to fly
Where graceful Eagles soar

Passion! Follow your passion! Those are words I have pondered time after time, year after year. Despite sporadic cogitation, I thought I'd never have a real passion for anything until late in life when I discovered I liked to write. Even then, writing wasn't a totally focused, all-consuming allurement for me.

On the other hand, my father, Kenneth Lee Chastain, did have a profound passion. His passion was flying. His love of aviation formed him as a person, drove his life, fulfilled him. In his later years he looked back with satisfaction. Born in the second decade of the twentieth century on September 20, 1913, it had been only ten years since the Wright Brothers flew their highly innovative, but fragile, flyer at Kitty Hawk, North Carolina. He was introduced to aviation in its infancy, at a time when flying was extremely dangerous, but very exciting.

It was 7:20 A.M. at his grandmother's home at 1012 3rd Avenue in Oakland, California, when my father came into the world. Nineteen thirteen was a time in U.S. history when significant events were taking place. Woodrow Wilson became President in March and in September the Sixteenth Amendment went into effect, providing for an income tax. The first tugboat passed through the Gatun Locks of the soon-to-be-completed Panama Canal, the Owens Valley Aqueduct opened bringing water to Los Angeles, and Hollywood became the center of the movie industry.

In 1913, multiple new companies were organized to build "aeroplanes" in addition to those already formed. At that point in time, aviation was only a miniscule part of the military. The U.S. Navy had seven planes and the U.S. Army had seventeen. Flying beyond the "straight and level" had been unheard of until that year when the first upside down maneuver and the first "loop" ever accomplished in the air were performed in a specially built Curtiss biplane.

My father's parents, Maryah Ann (Wann) and Everett Lee Chastain, lived in the Boyle Heights District of East Los Angeles, California. Kenneth was Ann's first child. Anxious, as many first-time mothers can be, she traveled all the way up to Oakland, California so she could give birth at her mother's (Lyzetta Ann Wann) house. After Kenneth's birth, Ann returned to her home in Southern California with her newborn son.

Living in the Los Angeles area greatly contributed to my father's exposure to flying because Southern California soon became a hotbed of aviation development. Southern California's moderate climate and affluent businessmen came together like a magnet, attracting such aviation pioneers as Jack Northrop, the Loughead (Lockheed) brothers, and Donald Douglas. In 1913, the Los Angeles basin was a rural area and its agricultural land ideal for use as rudimentary landing fields. One of those rural airports, Mines Field, would later be named Los Angeles International Airport (LAX).

On January 1, 1914, when my father was still in diapers, the St. Petersburg-Tampa Airboat Line began operations as the world's first scheduled airline using winged aircraft rather than the lighter-than-air dirigibles used by Germany. Nineteen fourteen also ushered in several exciting developments in aviation. The gyrocompass and the automatic pilot were invented and the first two-way radio communication took place between an airplane and the ground, in Manila. To that point in the history of American aviation, U.S. manufacturers had delivered only one hundred commercial and military aeroplanes.

Anthony Dewitt Pyeatt, the future friend, fellow model airplane builder, and brother of my father's future wife, was born on September 19, 1915, in San Bernardino, California. Dewitt eventually worked as an engineer for Donald Douglas' company, Douglas Aircraft, designing elements of two famous airplane types.

Nineteen fifteen saw the establishment of the National Advisory Committee for Aeronautics (NACA), which eventually became NASA. William E. Boeing became interested in aeronautics and began taking flying instructions at Glenn L. Martin's school in California. Boeing began building planes the next year. The company's first product, its Model 1, was a twin-pontoon, open-cockpit biplane. Designed as a utility aircraft, it accommodated two persons seated in tandem. Also in 1916, for the first time ever, airplanes in flight communicated with each other directly by radio.

It would be ten more years before my father would be introduced to the world of flying. Even though he was too young to be involved in aviation during that period of his life, aeronautical inventions, developments, and events were rapidly taking place that would greatly affect his future. On September 3, 1916, Ann gave birth to a daughter, Evelyn Maureen. My father was no longer an only child. The Chastain family lived in East Los Angeles through 1917.

On April 6, 1917, the United States entered the Great War, which was to become known as World War I (WWI). At the time of America's entry into WWI, the U.S. Army Signal Corps had 35 pilots and 55 training planes. The U.S. Navy had 38 pilots and 54 airplanes. This was a sad beginning; however, aviation development would be catapulted forward beyond anyone's imagination because of the war and the focused effort it provided for the advancement of aeronautics—a harbinger of things to come in the developing aviation industry.

An armistice was signed in November of 1918. During the short period the United States was involved in the war, the Army Air Service grew to 3,538 airplanes in the American Expeditionary Forces (A.E.F.) in Europe and 4,865 additional planes in the United States. Naval aviation grew to 2,127 airplanes, a few of which were land planes, but most were seaplanes.

In 1918, my father moved with his family to Deming, New Mexico for about a year. His father, Everett, had taken a job running the Deming Ice Cream Factory. While living there, both of my father's parents became ill with the flu. This was during the deadliest epidemic in world history—the great 1918 influenza outbreak. At the time it was called the "Spanish flu." In the space of months, tens of millions of people all over the world perished in agony. They died in only a matter of days or weeks. A great majority of the victims were young adults in the prime of their lives. Although the true death toll is unknown, it may have topped 100 million souls.

Many times more than that number contracted the disease, but survived. Fortunately, my father's parents were among the survivors, even though they were in the highest-risk group—people in their mid-to-late twenties. From her sick bed, Ann had my then five-year-old father light their kerosene stove to heat barley water for his newborn baby brother, Russell. Because of her illness, Ann couldn't nurse her baby. She prayed the stove wouldn't blow up, which fortunately, it didn't.

On October 12, 1918, my father's future wife, my mother, Lorraine Mercedes Pyeatt, was born on 2nd Street in San Bernardino, California.

In 1919, my father was six years old and living in the town of Coalinga in the Great Central Valley of California. The name "Coalinga" was derived from its days as Coaling Station A for the railroad (therefore "Coaling A" or "Coalinga.") Everett had taken a job as a carpenter with Pacific Oil, Plant 25. The only house available to them had one room, a dirt floor and outdoor toilets. The first thing Everett did was to use his skills as a carpenter and put in a floor.

As adults, the Chastain children remembered Coalinga as a beautiful place with hills filled with wildflowers. Even though they were poor, they thought of this period of their life as a "fun time." Everett and Ann had lots of friends there. On Saturday nights all of the people gathered at the one and only clubhouse. The men and women would either dance or play cards and the children would crawl onto the pool tables and go to sleep.

Many significant things occurred in 1919 that influenced both my father's and the country's future. Three things were established that would cause consternation over time for a great many people: the ratification of the Eighteenth Amendment to the U.S. Constitution establishing Prohibition, the founding of the American Communist Party, and the start of a fascist group in Italy by Mussolini and his cronies. The first municipal airport in the United States was dedicated in 1919 in Atlantic City, New Jersey, and the Navy Department announced that all first- and second-class American battleships were to be equipped with catapult-launched seaplanes.

When my father was just beginning grammar school, the reversible propeller was being tested at McCook Field, the Army Air Service's primary testing facility in Dayton, Ohio. By being able to reverse the propeller, airplanes could come to a stop more quickly. Other notable technical achievements reviewed at McCook Field in 1919 included leak-proof gas tanks, parachutes folded in a soft pack to be worn on the back, and a General Electric-developed supercharger.

On May 6, 1919, three U.S. Navy Curtiss flying boats took off from U.S. Naval Air Station Rockaway, New York in "V" formation. The flagship NC-3 was flanked by NC-1 and NC-4. They were embarking on the first transatlantic crossing by a heavier-than-air craft. Both NC-1 and NC-3 dropped out mid-ocean and the crews were rescued. This left the NC-4 to become the first aircraft of any kind to fly across the Atlantic Ocean, or for that matter, any ocean. Flying from New York via Massachusetts, Halifax, Nova Scotia, Newfoundland, and the Azores the crew reached Lisbon, Portugal on May 27.

The U.S. Navy's feat of making the first transatlantic flight was soon eclipsed by a pair of British aviators flying a Vickers Vimy biplane. Taking off from Newfoundland, they flew to Ireland on June 14 and 15, 1919. Flight time was 16 hours and 27 minutes.

"Eddie" Stinson, a former Army Air Services instructor and test pilot for Curtiss, formed a company in 1919 to develop and produce an enclosed-cabin airplane. Stinson Aircraft germinated from what was initially a family-owned flying school. Eddie's flight instructor sisters, Katherine and Marjorie, played major roles in running the business. Later in life my father worked for a Stinson distributor flying customer planes to analyze difficulties, as well as test flying all newly-assembled or repaired aircraft.

In the meantime, my father and his siblings were accumulating what they looked back on as many good memories in Coalinga. These were simple remembrances like gathering bouquets in the vast fields of colorful wildflowers surrounding the town.

In 1920, America was trying to return to a normal life after experiencing the horrors of WWI and at the same time, because of Prohibition, millions of Americans were breaking the law. The age of radio began in 1920. Americans spent one million dollars on radio sets.

Warren Harding became President in 1921. He was the first President-elect to ride to his inauguration in an automobile. In July of that year, Brigadier General William "Billy" Mitchell's planes sank a captured German battleship and other vessels in the Chesapeake Bay, emphatically showing the vulnerability of naval ships to attack from the air. My father gained a third sibling when his second sister, Neita, was born on January 3.

Also in 1921, Donald Douglas teamed up with David Davis to design and build a first-ever non-stop, coast-to-coast airplane. The resultant aircraft was dubbed the Cloudster. Douglas' partner Davis was more than just a wealthy Southern California sportsman and aviation enthusiast. He would later design and hold patents for an innovative, high-lift airfoil called the Davis Wing. During WWII it would be mass-produced for the B-24 Liberator bomber.

After two years and three failed attempts at flying cross country non-stop, Davis sold his interest in the venture. Donald Douglas, after a significant struggle to obtain backing, was able to obtain bare-bones financing and organize the Douglas Company in Los Angeles. The first aircraft built by the company in quantity was a military version of the Cloudster, designated DT-2. Forty were built for the U.S. Navy as torpedo planes in 1922 and 1923 (thus the designation DT for Douglas Torpedo). Later, aircraft built by Douglas Aircraft would figure prominently in my father's career as a pilot.

After WWI, war surplus aircraft flooded the commercial market. As a result, aircraft companies building for the civilian market struggled, and fought for the few military contracts available. At the time, only 1,200 commercial aircraft were operating in all of the United States, and from a mere 146 airfields.

On February 22, 1921, the first day and night cross-continental mail flights began. Prior to this the coast-to-coast mail was flown during the day and traveled on the railroad at night. The U.S. Congress funding airmail service was not impressed and hesitated to fund monies for expansion. Therefore, the attempt was made to make all legs of the journey by aircraft to speed up service. Two DH-4Bs were used in the effort. They were variants of the de Havilland 4 "Liberty Plane" developed for use in WWI.

Taking off simultaneously, one plane departed from San Francisco and the second from New York, embarking on America's first scheduled long distance flights. Both day and night, U.S. Air Mail Service pilots, flying wire-braced, open-cockpit biplanes, battled weather and darkness, making the trips in a little over 25 hours. As a result, Congress appropriated the necessary funding, establishing a pattern that would evolve into the present global air transportation network.

In 1922, the year the Lincoln Memorial was dedicated, my father's dad was offered one-half interest in his brother's truck and ice route in Los Angeles. These were the days of iceboxes, before the development of refrigerators. Everett accepted and the family moved back to Southern California. He delivered ice for Merchant's Ice and Cold Storage Company.

Nineteen twenty-two was also the year the first play-by-play coverage of the World Series was carried on the radio. In the military, the Navy's first aircraft carrier, the USS *Langley*, was commissioned in Norfolk, Virginia. In aviation the first experimental helicopters were introduced to America. First was the independently developed Berliner helicopter in June of that year. In December the DeBothezat helicopter, developed at McCook Field for the Army Air Service, hovered to a height of six feet. Neither of these early attempts was developed much further due to severe controllability issues and waning interest.

In 1923, the Chastain family moved in with Ann's parents, Lyzetta and John Wann. They lived in a small, three-room house with outside toilets. The house was located on Rosecrans and Sepulveda in Los Angeles, about one mile from the shore. The children made many trips to the beach, following the railroad tracks so Ann could easily find them. Ten people lived in that very small house. Besides my father, there were his grandparents, Lyzetta and John Wann, his parents, his two sisters and brother, his mother's brother, Ralph, and Ralph's son, Irvine.

Even though John Wann worked as a guard at a chemical plant near home and Everett was starting a new job as an ice deliveryman, the family had little money. To help them get by, they grew a large vegetable garden. The family also worked together to make taffy candy, which they sold to the neighbors. The children learned if they didn't eat what was on their plate at dinner it was there for them the next morning for breakfast. Because things were bad financially, you had to eat what you were given.

Water was very scarce, too. On Saturday nights, Lyzetta placed a large tub in the kitchen. She filled it with water she had heated on the stove, after which all of the children were given a bath, one at a time. They started with Neita because she was the youngest and worked up in age from there. The same water was used for all, but hot water was added as needed.

In Washington, D.C., Calvin Coolidge gave the first presidential speech to be broadcast by radio in an address to Congress. The Army Air Service ordered its aircrews to wear parachutes at all times during flight and the first nonstop transcontinental flight was made from Long Island, New York to San Diego, California in an ungainly Fokker T-2 transport aircraft. Also over San Diego, the first mid-air refueling was made between two aircraft.

In 1924, when there were 2.5 million radios in the United States, Ann rented a duplex on Rowan Avenue in Los Angeles. She didn't tell the landlord she had children, so she sneaked them in at night. They only stayed a month because keeping the children quiet was too difficult for her.

Like a train pulling out of a station, the story of aviation had begun to embark on a journey that would change the world forever. My father hadn't yet jumped aboard, but that would soon change. An event epitomizing this took place on March 17, 1924, when four DWC aircraft took off from Clover Field in Santa Monica and headed for Alaska via Seattle. The planes belonged to the Army Air Service whose pilots were looking to be the first to circumnavigate the globe.

The aircraft were built by Donald Douglas' new company especially for this attempt. The official Air Service designation was Douglas World Cruiser (DWC) and one, the *Chicago*, is preserved today in the National Air & Space Museum in Washington, D.C. (See photo at the end of this chapter). Four of these single-engine biplanes took off from Seattle on April 6, flown by the United States Air Service's best pilots. It took the two planes that were successful 175 days and many stops along the way to complete the journey.

In 1925, the Nation's first motel opened in Monterey, California and A&W became the first fast-food franchise, pointing to the fact automobiles were now a force to be heeded in America. In aviation, the U.S. Navy's small but awe-inspiring dirigible fleet took a hit when the USS *Shenandoah* (ZR-1) was torn apart and crashed in an Ohio storm. And in an event with great significance for the future, the Postmaster General was authorized to contract airmail routes with private operators.

My father was 12 years old in 1925 when he got his first job, which was delivering newspapers. Being the oldest of four children and coming from a poor family, he learned some valuable lessons he would carry with him for life. For instance, he voluntarily shared his earnings with his brother and sisters. He wasn't yet aware of it, but the dawning of his future career in aviation was just over the horizon.

Kenneth in front of a Douglas World Cruiser aircraft, the Chicago
(National Air & Space Museum, 1990)

Chapter 2
Entrée to Aviation

The nation's financial engine sputtered
While Lindbergh challenged the sky
Conquering the mighty Atlantic Ocean
And empowering the world to fly

The year 1926 was a watershed year. In a period of time when significant events were taking place annually, this mid-decade year stood out for the world, the country, aviation, and for my father. It was the year Prince Hirohito succeeded to the throne in Japan after the death of his father and Richard Byrd flew over the North Pole in a tri-motored Fokker airplane *Josephine Ford,* named after Edsel Ford's daughter. NBC began radio network broadcasting for the first time and Robert Goddard launched the first liquid-fueled rocket in Massachusetts. President Calvin Coolidge signed the Civilian Aviation Act, establishing the Bureau of Air Commerce, which licensed both aircraft and pilots.

My father was about to jump on board the "Aviation Express." He was in the seventh grade at Robert Louis Stevenson Junior High School in Los Angeles. During this time, his Sunday school teacher gave him the book *The ABCs of Flight.*

Later in life he would credit the reading of that book as the event which began his interest in aviation. He had been aware of airplanes before that time, but hadn't really connected flying to himself. He began thinking about how he could get involved with this new and exciting endeavor.

On January 25, 1926, the company Eddie Stinson founded in 1919 rolled out the Stinson SM-1 for its maiden flight. It was the first of a new product line of monoplanes dubbed the Detroiter. It was an overnight success. Also in that year two new aircraft manufacturing companies were founded. Like Stinson, they would end up playing a part in my father's future in aviation.

First was Stearman Aircraft, Inc. It was initially formed in Venice, California on October 1926. For financial reasons production was halted and on September 27, 1927, a new Stearman Aircraft Corporation was founded with a factory in Wichita, Kansas. Not many years afterward, my father would spend numerous hours plying the skies in open cockpit Stearman biplanes.

Second the Loughead (Lockheed) brothers started an airplane manufacturing company in Burbank, California. It was incorporated on December 17, 1926, as the Lockheed Aircraft Company. On July 4, 1927, the first of Lockheed's Vega series aircraft, named the *Golden Eagle*, took off from the Los Angeles factory. The Vega was destined to be flown in several record breaking flights. My father would work for Lockheed later in his life where, among other tasks, he supervised engine installation on the famous Lockheed Electra.

My father's interest in aviation couldn't have peaked at a more auspicious time, for in 1927 aviation took several giant steps forward in achievement. In May, Charles A. Lindbergh became the first person to fly solo, nonstop across the Atlantic Ocean. He flew his plane the *Spirit of St. Louis* over 3,600 miles from New York to Paris, picking up a $25,000 prize and becoming a national hero along the way. A copy of the book *The Boy's Story of Lindbergh: the Lone Eagle* remained in my father's possession all of his life.

The spigot to long distance flight was now open. In early June 1927, two pilots flew their Bellanca monoplane, *Columbia*, nonstop from New York to Germany. Later that same month two Army Lieutenants flew a Fokker tri-motor, *Bird of Paradise*, from Oakland Municipal Airport, California and made the first transpacific crossing to Wheeler Field, Oahu, Hawaii.

On August 25, 1927, 25-year-old Paul Redfern took off from Brunswick, Georgia flying a Stinson Detroiter SM-1 in an attempt to fly nonstop to Rio de Janeiro. The plane was painted green and yellow—the colors in Brazil's flag. The president of Brazil and movie star Clara Bow planned to greet him upon his arrival. He never arrived and was presumed lost at sea. If he had been successful he would have flown 1000 miles farther than Charles Lindbergh did in his flight to Paris three months earlier. A Street in Ipanema is named after him.

It was 1927 when an Army Lieutenant named James Doolittle performed the first "outside loop" ever accomplished in an airplane. It was also the year Henry Ford showed the first Model A to the public, replacing the old Tin Lizzie or Model T, and when the first television broadcast was beamed from the New York headquarters of AT&T showing Secretary of Commerce Herbert Hoover speaking from his Washington office. The first "talking" motion picture was released in that year featuring the singing of Al Jolson.

The Everett Chastain family decided to move from the "city" (Los Angeles) to the "country" in Monterey Park. Coincident with the family moving to 522 East Emerson Avenue in Monterey Park, the Cessna Aircraft Company was being formed in Wichita, Kansas. It closed its doors after the stock market crash of 1929, but was later reopened to become the worldwide success it is to this day.

While living in Monterey Park, my father attended the eighth grade at Garvey Grammar School. In later years, my father's sister, Evelyn, remembered that while attending Garvey school there were many children who had no shoes to wear because it was such a poor time. The Chastain children wore hand-me-downs, but at least they had shoes.

Nineteen twenty-seven was also when the Advance Aircraft Company brought out the Waco Ten. This three-seat open-cockpit biplane was found to have excellent handling characteristics and its pilots helped popularize flying by providing barnstorming and joyride flights to the public. The Waco Ten was one of many aircraft types my father later flew.

Nineteen twenty-eight was the year Amelia Earhart became the first woman to fly the Atlantic Ocean as a passenger in the Fokker tri-motor *Friendship*. The first color motion picture was demonstrated by George Eastman in Rochester, New York and the motion picture *Wings* won the very first Academy Award for best picture. Additionally, Richard Byrd and three other aviators became the first to fly over the South Pole in a monoplane named *Floyd Bennett*.

In 1928, my father began attending Alhambra High School and found a way to become involved in aviation. By working part-time after school and on weekends at Callies Field in Monterey Park, he learned how to work on both aircraft and their engines. He worked under the supervision of a very experienced, old-time barnstorming pilot, Art Callies. This experience was extremely valuable because at that point in the development of aviation, pilots not only had to know how to fly an airplane, but also how to repair the planes they flew. In those days, reliability was not an aircraft's strong suit.

My father, like so many other boys influenced by Charles Lindbergh, began building model airplanes, a hobby he would continue throughout his entire lifetime. There weren't any kits, plans or dedicated materials with which to build models when he started. Such things simply didn't exist. He and other young model builders made their own designs and learned by trial and error how to make an airplane fly. There were many crack-ups.

The National Air Races were held in Los Angeles in 1928, adding to my father's excitement about airplanes, and while he was getting his hands dirty with grease from engine work, several new aircraft types were being introduced that he would fly later in life. Among those were the Consolidated Fleet biplane, the Aeronca C-3 monoplane, the Kari Keene Koupe monoplane and the Aeromarine Klemm monoplane.

When the Stock Market crashed in 1929, its effects led to the worst depression in history. For the most part, it didn't slow the development of aviation or my father's involvement in it. In September, First Lieutenant James H. "Jimmy" Doolittle made the world's first flight solely on instruments. His airplane used an artificial horizon and a directional gyroscope made by Elmer Sperry, a sensitive altimeter made by Paul Kollsman, and radio equipment from the National Bureau of Standards. Flying completely blind using the navigational instruments provided, Doolittle took off from Mitchell Field on Long Island, flew for fifteen miles, then returned, making a perfect landing.

My father joined the Monterey Park Glider Club that year. He was sixteen years old. Each club member flew, maintained, and repaired the club's Evans Primary Glider. According to my father, there were lots of repairs to be made because they would often dip a wing and ground loop (i.e., make a violent turn). They flew in the Shandon Hills behind San Bernardino, California.

While my father was beginning to sprout his wings, other notable events were taking place in aviation. The first in-flight movie was shown on a flight from Minneapolis to Chicago. The German dirigible *Graf Zeppelin* flew around the world, covering

19,500 miles in just over twenty-one days, and the first transcontinental air service was begun, flying from New York to Los Angeles. It took thirty-six hours, including one overnight stop.

On a more personal note, because of my father's developing interest in music, his mother bought him a Conn trumpet. Even though times were tough, she spent $115.50 for it and paid it off in $10.50 installments.

Outstanding developments in aviation in 1929 included practical wing flaps and an engine cowling for air-cooled, radial engines. Also, Nicholas-Beazley, an aircraft supply house in Marshall, Missouri, entered the aircraft construction business with their NB-3. This was the forerunner of the plane in which my father soloed. Other new developments demonstrated that year were color television and FM radio.

In the summer of 1930, my father began helping his dad deliver ice for California Consumer Corporation. Everett started work at 3 A.M. His route was in Los Angeles, running from the 3rd Street tunnel to Crown Hill. The Crown Hill area was filled with two- and three-story apartment buildings. With no elevators to assist him, Everett carried heavy blocks of ice on his back up all of those stairwells, holding on with just a set of tongs. For two years my father helped out whenever he wasn't in school, earning $1,000.00 per year.

The planet Pluto was discovered that year, which was a scientifically exciting event, but Americans were firmly planted on Earth and beginning to feel the effects of the 1929 stock market crash. There were 1,300 bank failures in 1930. Delivering ice was hard work, but it was work and work was becoming harder to come by as the Great Depression affected more and more people.

In 1930 a new profession was added to the young aviation industry. A registered nurse and student pilot, Ellen Church, became the first airline stewardess for the newly formed United Airlines. Church was asked to recruit seven more nurses. In order to be considered, the candidate had to be 25 years of age and single, have a "pleasant personality," and be no taller than 5 feet, 4 inches, nor weigh more than 115 pounds. These new stewardesses served cold meals and beverages and calmed any passenger suffering from the fear of flying.

It was in 1930 that the aviation industry's trend toward substituting metal for wood in aircraft construction began in earnest. It was also the year that Frank Whittle, a British engineer, patented the jet engine.

On June 7, 1931, my father logged his first flight in an Evans Secondary glider. He had made 62 flights prior to this without recording them. The flight took place in the Shandon Hills and lasted one minute, forty-five seconds. While my father was busy flying gliders, the Buhl Aircraft Company started building the Buhl Pup and the Taylor Aircraft Company began building the Taylor Cub, two airplane types my father was destined to fly.

Even though the world kept progressing with things like the opening of the Empire State Building in New York and the development of a stereophonic sound system by Bell Laboratories, the Great Depression continued to deepen. Several aircraft manufacturers succumbed to it that year and 2,294 more banks failed in the United States. In another ominous occurrence, the very first step was taken down the road to World War II when the Japanese Army seized Manchuria.

Still little affected by these events, my father continued flying gliders in the Shandon Hills, the Monterey Park Glider Field, the Garvey Hills, Hollywood Riviera in Redondo, and the Fullerton Hills. He obtained an early Department of Commerce Glider License (No. 413) on October 9, 1931. He mostly flew his club's Evans Glider (I.D. G125W), but he also took one flight in a primary glider built by the Crown City Glider Club and test flew a Rhon Ranger primary glider for its owners. He continued flying gliders until January 3, 1932, when, ironically, Air Commerce Regulations governing gliders and gliding became effective.

The Great Depression reached an all time low in 1932 with the Dow Jones Average hitting bottom at 41.22. This was a 90 percent loss of value from its September 1929 peak of 381.17. With 13.7 million people unemployed in the United States, the hit song of the day was "Brother, Can You Spare a Dime?" That year, several more aircraft companies either went into receivership or closed down, and the Japanese heavily bombed China's largest city, Shanghai, killing or wounding thousands of civilians.

In 1932, my father began working at Alhambra Airport as an apprentice under the Airport Manager, Lou Rous. He made 25 cents an hour after school and on weekends working for plane owners, servicing and cleaning their aircraft. He also made minor repairs on their planes under the supervision of licensed aircraft mechanics.

In May 1932, on the fifth anniversary of Charles Lindbergh's epoch flight from New York to Paris and four years after becoming the first woman to fly the Atlantic Ocean as a passenger, Amelia Earhart became the first female pilot to fly solo across the Atlantic. She battled electrical storms, severe icing and mechanical glitches as she flew her single engine Lockheed Vega from St. Johns, New Brunswick to Londonderry, Ireland. Afterward, "Lady Lindy" tasted some of Lindbergh's fame.

In August, Amelia set a long distance record for a woman pilot, while at the same time becoming the first female pilot to fly non-stop across the United States. It took her a little over nineteen hours to fly from Los Angeles, California to Newark, New Jersey.

While all of this was going on, my father began flying powered airplanes himself, pulling weeds at the airport to pay for flying lessons. His first dual flight was in a Nicholas Beazley NB-

8. On July 17, 1932, he soloed in NB-8 (registration number NC542Y) out of Sprott Airport in East Los Angeles. World War I pilot, Major Bryan of Bryan Flying Service, owned the plane. My father continued flying solo in NB-8s for the balance of the year.

Kenneth in one of his gliders at age 16 (1929)

Kenneth with the Nicholas Beazley NB-8 in which he soloed. Photo taken at Sprott Airport in East Los Angeles, California (1932)

Chapter 3
Mercedes

He grew, matured and took his vows
With the girl of his dreams
While Nazis honed their skills of war
To anguished Spanish screams

My father had a good friend he had met at Alhambra Airport named Dewitt Pyeatt. He and Dewitt were both interested in aviation and built model airplanes together. One evening when they decided to go to the movies, Dewitt's parents insisted he take his sister with them. He did and my father met Lorraine Mercedes Pyeatt, his future wife and my mother.

This was 1933, the year of the great "unnamed" earthquake. Both Mercedes and Dewitt came down with typhoid fever and were in bed when the quake occurred. Later in life, Dewitt recalled how the beds they were in slid around the room as the earth shook. Because both he and his sister had typhoid fever, the house was quarantined for about a month; however, during that time my father crawled in the bedroom window, supposedly to visit his friend, Dewitt, but I'm sure it was Mercedes he really wanted to see.

My father graduated from Alhambra High School in June as part of the summer class of 1933. The romance between Mercedes and him quickly ignited as evidenced by her message to him in his class yearbook:

MY OWN DARLING BOY,

YOU TOLD ME NOT TO WRITE IN THIS BOOK, BUT I'M GOING TO BE A BAD GIRL AND DO IT ANYWAY. PLEASE DON'T SPANK ME.

I NOTICE A CERTAIN PERSON ADDRESSED YOU AS 'DARLING' IN THIS BOOK, BUT WHEN I ADDRESS YOU IN SUCH A MANNER, I'M TRULY SINCERE.

I WISHED AFTER I HAD STARTED GOING WITH YOU THAT I'D HAD THE PRIVILEGE OF GOING THROUGH SCHOOL WITH YOU AND I STILL WISH I HAD AND ALSO I WISH I HAD BEEN BORN IN THE SAME ROOM WITH YOU, PLAYED IN THE SAME STREETS WITH YOU, BUT IT'S TOO LATE NOW. NEVER-THE-LESS WE'RE TOGETHER NOW AND FOR ALWAYS. I'M WAITING IMPATIENTLY FOR THE TIME WHEN WE BOTH SAY TOGETHER, 'I DO,' AND SWEETHEART, WHEN THAT TIME COMES YOU CAN JUST BET YOUR LIFE THAT I'LL BE THE MOST HAPPY GIRL IN THIS WHOLE WIDE WORLD.

SINCERELY AND FOREVER,
YOUR OWN, MERCEDES

One time my father flew over Merc's house and dropped a note to her in a small, silk parachute. He kept that parachute for many years afterward.

As he left high school my father entered a rapidly changing world. On March 4, 1933, Franklin D. Roosevelt was inaugurated President of the United States. At just the right moment in history, the country elected a leader with his hand on America's pulse and the wherewithal to inject a sense of energy and action into the psyche of the American people. In his first one hundred days in office, a quick succession of Congressional bills was passed, including emergency banking reform, the Federal Emergency Relief Act, the National Industrial Recovery Act, and the creation of the Civilian Conservation Corps. The first steps had been taken to seriously address the effects of the Great Depression.

On the other side of the Atlantic, Adolph Hitler was sworn in as Chancellor of Germany. Shortly thereafter, a humbled Reichstag gave Hitler the authority to legislate by decree. By summer of that year, Nazi power was supreme and the world was headed toward the brink of disaster.

The U.S. Navy Aircraft Carrier USS *Ranger* (CV-4) was launched on February 25, 1933 in Newport News, Virginia. It was the first ship designed from the keel up as an aircraft carrier. The first three carriers, USS *Langley* (CV-1), USS *Lexington* (CV-2), and USS *Saratoga* (CV-3) had all been converted from other types of ships. In future years, I would be a crew member of the submarine USS *James Monroe* (SSBN-622) when it was commissioned at the Newport News shipyard.

In April, British aviators became the first to fly over the "roof of the world"—Mount Everest—piloting Westland PV-3 open-cabin biplanes. The extreme altitude conditions of air temperature, pressure and reduced oxygen supply experienced by the crews helped demonstrate the need for pressurized cabins in modern aircraft.

The National Air Races, sponsored by the National Aeronautical Association, were again held in Los Angeles July 1 through 4, 1933. Colonel and Mrs. Charles Lindbergh, flying a Lockheed Sirius seaplane, made a 29,000-mile air route survey flight from New York to Labrador, Greenland, Iceland, Europe, the Azores, Africa, Brazil, and back. Anne Morrow Lindbergh wrote a book on part of the trip called *Listen! The Wind*. This book also became a part of my father's lifelong library.

Nineteen thirty-three was the year that Douglas Aircraft designed the DC-1 transport aircraft for Transcontinental and

Western Air. The DC-1 was a prototype to the DC-2 and later DC-3 transports. The DC-3 and its military counterpart played an important role in my father's flying career.

After high school my father was unable to obtain a job, so on September 14 he joined the United States Army Air Corps and was stationed at March Field near Riverside, California. The Post Commander was Lieutenant Colonel Henry "Hap" Arnold who would serve during World War II as Commanding General, Army Air Forces.

Dad was attached to the 11th Bomb Squadron of the 7th Bomb Group. His salary was $21.00 per month at first. After President Roosevelt's New Deal was initiated, he took a 15 percent pay cut, so as a Buck Private, he made $17.85 per month. He was assigned to the Aero Repair Section and did all types of aircraft and engine service, maintenance, and repair, including line service and crew chief. Because he was also able to play the trumpet, he became one of March Field's buglers.

Nineteen thirty-three was also the year Congress repealed the Eighteenth Amendment to the Constitution. The country concluded the "noble experiment" had been a disastrous mistake, and the demise of Prohibition was quickly ratified by the states.

In March 1933 plastic was inadvertently synthesized at Imperial Chemical Industries in Great Britain. An unknown commodity at the time, it was destined to become an integral part of everyday life worldwide.

Having soloed the previous year and accumulated the requisite number of flying hours, my father received his Department of Commerce pilot's license (Number 28686) on March 14, 1933. He flew six airplane types in 1933. He continued flying Nicholas Beazley NB-8s. He also flew the stubby, high-winged Aeronca C-3 monoplane, the single low-wing Aeromarine Klemm, the Travel Air 2000, the Consolidated Fleet biplane and the Buhl Bull Pup monoplane.

My father had what was to be his only airplane accident in 1934. It took place in a Waco 10 belonging to his friend, Forrest Wiley. It was a taxiing accident where a pilot taxiing in an Alexander Eaglerock ran into the Waco. The wings collided, causing the planes to swing around so the propellers ran into each other, destroying them. This caused the Waco's engine to vibrate radically until my father could shut it down. The other pilot was found to be at fault.

October 20, 1934, was Mercedes Pyeatt's 16th birthday. On that day she and my father scurried away to Yuma, Arizona where Judge E.A. Freeman married them. Judge Freeman was known at that time as "the marrying judge." Mercedes lied about her age, so the marriage certificate listed her age as 18 years old. Except for telling Merc's mother, Cleo Pyeatt, the marriage was kept under wraps—after all, my father was in the Army and living on base.

In December 1934, the 7th Bombardment Group was moved north to Hamilton Field in Marin County, California. The base, located approximately twenty miles north of San Francisco, was named in honor of First Lieutenant Lloyd Andrews Hamilton, who was killed in action in France during World War I. My father was among the first of the personnel transferred to this new Army Air Corps field. With a new wife in Southern California and all of his flying connections there as well, he wasn't very happy about being stuck up north.

Lockheed Aircraft Corporation started producing the ten-passenger, all-metal Electra in 1934. The Electra and Douglas Aircraft's DC-2 were two of the first transport planes to incorporate landing flaps. The Electra was the plane Amelia Earhart used in her failed attempt to circumnavigate the world. It also played a part in my father's aviation life.

In 1934, my father added five new plane types to the list of planes he had flown. He flew the Waco 10 in which he had his only accident. He flew the high-wing Kari Keen monoplane, as well as the Stinson SM-8A "Junior" and the J-2 Taylor Cub (precursor to the Piper Cub). The fifth airplane type he flew that year was a Curtiss-Wright Junior. This must have been a fairly old airplane even then because it was powered by a three-cylinder Szekly pusher engine.

The dangers of flying were brought home to my father that year. He was flying through clear skies over Southern California one day and looked down on the open fields near Sprott Airport and smiled. With the fresh, clean air of 1930s California hitting him in the face, he was in his element—a man alone, aloft and soaring. The steady hum of the English-made Genet engine instilled confidence in him for his craft. He relished looking out of his single-wing NB-8, watching the wide, empty fields surrounding East Los Angeles pass him by below. He flew over his parents' house in Monterey Park, circling lazily in the bright, blue, cloudless sky, wondering if they would notice him.

What a wonderful day for flying, but what day wasn't? After all, flying was becoming his life. Like the conscientious flyer he was, he checked his fuel level. *Better be heading back to the airport,* he thought. He hated it when he had to land. Flying for him was a high that could not be duplicated in any other way. He was aware that aviation was young, but so was he. The planes were fragile, even dangerous, but he knew in his gut nothing would happen to him. He was too careful, too cautious.

Lining his plane up with the wide, dirt landing strip, he came in smoothly, gliding to a perfect three-point landing. The propeller kicked up dust from the strip as he taxied over to the hangar. After shutting down the engine he waved to Major Bryan's girlfriend as he climbed out of the open cockpit. He didn't know her well, but he felt it was important to be friendly with everyone, especially the girlfriend of the owner of the plane he was flying. He had even soloed in that plane.

After arranging to have the plane refueled, he went into the hangar to check the progress being made on the Aeronca C-3 being refitted. He was studying to be an Aircraft and Engines Mechanic as well as honing his skills as a pilot. He was so interested in aviation and every facet of it intrigued him.

A couple of hours after he had landed, his good friend Dewitt left the airport administration building and walked over to the Nicholas Beazley NB-8 my father had just flown. Dewitt, too, must have figured it was a beautiful day for a flight. Knowing Major Bryan rented his plane out to others, "Dee" seemed ready to take it up for a spin. After making the usual pre-flight checks and switching the ignition switch on, he walked up to the prop and put his hands on the right side of the propeller to give it a pull start. Just as he was about to kick his right leg out for leverage and pull the blade down, someone grabbed him from behind and pulled him away with a jerk.

"What the . . . ?"

"Dee, that's an English engine." My father had come back out of the hangar and had seen what Dewitt was about to do. Dewitt was still suffering from the shock of being yanked away from the plane and didn't quite understand the gravity of what was being said to him.

"English engines start by pulling them to the left—counterclockwise. The way you were standing, if the engine caught, you could have been in deep trouble."

"Thanks buddy. I guess that was close!"

My father simply smiled in his understated way. "It's no big deal, just be aware." He then started the engine, showing Dewitt how it should be done.

His attention deflected, Dewitt walked back to the airport administration building, leaving his friend standing by the running engine. Major Bryan appeared at that moment and told my father he thought he'd take the NB-8 up for a spin. The World War I pilot used the plane as an added source of income.

"I think I'll do a few slow figure eights over the field and see if I can draw any customers in. We can use the business."

My father watched as the Major climbed into the small craft, strapped himself in and revved the engine for taxiing. Dust blew in his face and he turned his back against the slipstream of the turning plane. It didn't take long for the little NB-8 to reach the end of the primitive airstrip and quickly swing around into the wind. My father heard the Genet engine strain as the pilot upped the revolutions to check for any irregularities in its sound. Seemingly satisfied, the pilot released the brakes and the plane began to roll. Gathering speed, trailing a cloud of dust, the fragile craft took to the air. Suddenly, free from the drag of its wheels on the earth, the plane seemed to jump into the sky.

I wish I were up there, my father thought, but it was also enjoyable just to watch a professional handle his craft. His World War I flying experience made Major Bryan a skilled and polished aviator. My father watched as the Major painted imaginary figure eights in the heavens. *Oh, to fly like that . . . one day, one day.*

Suddenly, as my father watched, all tranquility vanished. He grimaced in horror. A wing of the NB-8 had fallen off. One minute the little plane was a picture of an airman's dream; the next, the nightmare all pilots dread. As the broken wing gently fluttered to earth, the rest of the NB-8 came spinning quickly down. Like a corkscrew, the crippled plane bore through the air on its way to the ground and then, with an awful thud, the horror of which can only be experienced but never described, it hit between the rails of the nearby railroad tracks, no more than ten or fifteen feet from the edge of the runway.

My father and Dewitt were among those who raced to the crumpled mass that was once a graceful airship. It was my father and Dewitt who had to face the reality of the death of their mentor, their hero. Only one word came to mind—horrible.

Major Bryan was dead, killed on impact; however, he had been a skilled pilot to the very end. He was still strapped in his harness, but had managed to turn off the engine ignition switch to prevent a fire. He had done everything he could have done before he hit. Trained and practiced reaction aside, without a parachute and with too little time to react, the inevitable had happened.

My father got the crumpled body of the Major out of his harness and off to the hospital, though his efforts were in vain. Dewitt had to get a Stevens truck to pull the plane's fuselage out from between the railroad tracks because it was so deeply imbedded. These actions were the natural reaction of flyers when tragedy strikes. Do something. Do anything. Just stay active and keep your mind off of the awful events at hand.

Why had the wing come off? Was the plane designed poorly? Was it maintained improperly? No. Because the plane was rented out to others, it was at the mercy of those who rented it. Someone had damaged the external strut fitting attached to the wing and tried to fix it by re-welding the joint—only whoever it was did a very bad job and it had cost the life of a vital human being, a human being who was loved by his girlfriend, a human being who was revered by Dewitt and my father.

My father had just flown that very airplane not two hours before. Fate spared his life that day. Fate was also on the side of Dewitt, who could have been without a leg, or worse, but who's to say what fate awaits one. In a single moment in time, all that is given can be either changed irrevocably or taken away forever. That day was a day just like the one before it. It was a day like the one that would follow—a beautiful, tranquil Southern California day. But that day would leave a lifelong imprint on at least three people. Throughout his life, Dewitt credited my father with saving his life.

On August 14, 1935, President Franklin Roosevelt signed the Social Security Act. Just one legislative act of several rising out of the New Deal, Americans still rely on Social Security to this day. Nineteen thirty-five was also the year a warning system called "radar" was devised.

Also in August, the very popular humorist, Will Rogers, was killed in an airplane crash while taking off near Point Barrow, Alaska. The plane had been piloted by Wiley Post, who was also killed. Just two years prior, Post had gained notoriety for his round-the-world flight in his Lockheed Vega.

Amelia Earhart became the first person to fly solo from Hawaii to California in 1935 and Major James Doolittle, with two passengers aboard, flew an American Airlines plane non-stop from Los Angeles to Brooklyn, New York in one minute less than twelve hours. This record wouldn't last very long, however, but the important thing was it was now easily possible to fly passengers from coast to coast.

My father had been taking night school courses in algebra, geometry, typing, and bookkeeping while stationed at March Field in Southern California. Because of that, he was able to convince the Army to transfer him back to March Field from Hamilton Field. He was transferred back in mid-1935 where he went to work for the Post Aircraft Inspector, Sergeant William C. Wagner. While in this job he inspected aircraft and aircraft parts on the Martin B-10 and B-12 bombers, the Boeing P-26 Peashooter fighter, and the B-2, B-4, BT-2, A-17, F1A, C-14, and C-27. That year he flew the Travel Air 2000, the Consolidated Fleet, the Kari Keen Koupe, the J-2 Taylor Cub and the Curtiss-Wright Junior.

In December 1935, Douglas Aircraft Company tested the new, all-metal, twin-engine DC-3. With its 21 seats, the new transport was "the first airplane in the world that could make money just by hauling passengers," according to American Airlines' President. The DC-3 would become the most popular and durable transport aircraft ever built. More than 10,000 were eventually manufactured for both military and commercial use. Hundreds of them are still flying today.

As a graduate from Muir Technical High School and Pasadena Junior College majoring in engineering, Dewitt was involved in Douglas Aircraft's design effort. He designed the brake mechanism for the main landing gear of the DC-3 so the wheels would stop turning after takeoff. He also engineered all of the aluminum castings in the DC-3's fuselage.

Nineteen thirty-five was also the year the Boeing Airplane Company produced the Model 299 four-engine bomber. This was the first of the Flying Fortress or B-17 type airplanes that would play such a crucial role for America in World War II.

In 1936, President Roosevelt was re-elected in a landslide victory. His innovative programs aimed at steering the nation out of the depths of the Depression were giving the people of America reason to hope. The New Deal's Work Projects Administration (WPA) even touched the field of aviation. In 1936 there were 40,000 men in 42 states working on $35,000,000 worth of aviation projects.

Elsewhere, the Spanish Civil War began in 1936, giving the German and Italian militaries a place to try out their new weapons of destruction from the air. Their planes supported General Francisco Franco's troops with hundreds of bombing missions. The most infamous raid, made by a squadron of German Heinkel 51 aircraft, destroyed the town of Guernica, killing sixteen hundred Spaniards and wounding eight hundred others.

On a more positive note, the Oakland Bay Bridge was completed that year, along with Boulder Dam on the Colorado River. Boulder Dam, later to be named "Hoover Dam," created Lake Mead, the largest reservoir in the world.

On February 16, 1936, the first Douglas Aircraft DST (Douglas Sleeper Transport) entered airline service. The daytime version of this airplane was called the DC-3. Lockheed Aircraft also began delivering its Electra, with the first three going to the U.S. Army Air Corps. Another went to Amelia Earhart for use as an aerial laboratory in conjunction with her work as Consultant Member of the Purdue University faculty.

The Nicholas Beazley NB-8 that lost its wing

Kenneth in a J-2 Taylor Cub (1935)

Kenneth and a friend in a Travelaire flying down to San Diego and over the border to Tijuana on a pleasure flight (1936)

The new soldier with a Stinson SM8-A at Alhambra Airport. Kenneth had just joined the USAAF (1933).

Kenneth in an Aeromarine Klemm (1933)

*Kenneth with a Trave-
laire 2000. He thought
the Travelaire was a good
plane (1933).*

Kenneth doing his homework. He was attending junior college classes in Riverside while in the Army, stationed at March Field (1936).

Lorraine Mercedes Pyeatt at age 15

Mercedes in Kenneth's graduation robe (1933)

Chapter 4
A&E Mechanic

The Allied Armies were in full retreat
As Blitzkrieg raged across the seas
But America came to Britain's aid
By gearing up its factories

A s of April 1936, just less than 15,000 flyers held active Department of Commerce pilot licenses. My father was one of those few, but he didn't stop there. That same year he also obtained a Department of Commerce A&E (Aircraft and Engines) Mechanics License (Number 14474) while still in the Army. In September, upon termination of his three-year Army enlistment, he was honorably discharged at March Field.

On July 6, 1936, for the first time, the federal government assumed control of the airlines' enroute air control facilities in Newark, Cleveland, and Chicago. That control eventually spread to all air traffic along the country's airways.

September was also the month the National Air Races were held at Mines Field in Los Angeles, California. Mines Field would later be named "Los Angeles International Airport." My father flew to the races in a Great Lakes biplane owned by Ed Bush. While there, he took a photograph of a Ford Tri-motor flying down the runway with one wheel on the ground. Although the plane in the photo looks as if it was about to crash, it didn't.

In October, my father went to work for Transcontinental & Western Air, Inc. (TWA) in Kansas City, Missouri as an A&E Mechanic. He was paid 60 cents an hour. Kansas City was the main terminal and overhaul base for TWA. He worked on aircraft and engines on DC-2, DC-3, and Ford 5AT aircraft. The Ford 5AT was also known as the Tri-Motor or the Tin Goose.

This is when my father finally told his parents and Merc's dad they were married. The truth came out when Merc went to Kansas City to be with my father. Up to that time they had been living separately. My father went first with my mother following "Non-Rev" (non-revenue) in a TWA DC-2. On the trip out she noticed the plane constantly yawed. It turned out DC-2s had a problem with the autopilot, causing a constant yaw. The DC-3 had an improved autopilot which didn't exhibit the same condition.

In Kansas City my parents lived in an apartment above a beauty shop at 3911 South Troost. They stayed there until February 1937 when Transcontinental transferred my father to their Winslow, Arizona station. While in Winslow he served as lead mechanic. He had four mechanics working under him troubleshooting grounded aircraft. He also did routine servicing and ensured the airport was properly maintained.

During the summer of 1937, my father's sister-in-law, Nita Pyeatt, came to Winslow to spend the summer with her sister, Mercedes. She spent three months there. One night during that time, Nita and my parents went out with my parent's landlord, Pat Williams. They spent the evening drinking champagne. After a while my mother and Nita decided they wanted to dance. However, when they went to stand up, their legs were too shaky to dance due to the effects of the champagne. Nita was sixteen and my mother was nineteen. Alcohol was a new experience for them.

Nineteen thirty-seven was the year Japan invaded China, starting a bloody, eight-year war with that country. On the other side of the world, German bombers, in support of General Francisco Franco, destroyed the Spanish town of Guernica. This horrific event prodded Pablo Picasso to paint *Guernica*, one of the twentieth century's most famous paintings.

The young field of aviation also suffered in 1937. Two tragedies took place that shook the country. In May, the German dirigible *Hindenburg* caught fire and exploded as it was approaching a mooring tower in Lakehurst, New Jersey. While an emotional radio announcer described the event, it was filmed and recorded for posterity. Thirty-six people died and many others were seriously injured. This horrible disaster sounded the death knell for regular passenger service by lighter-than-air craft.

The second tragic event took place on July 2, when the 39-year-old pilot Amelia Earhart, while attempting an around-the-world flight, took off from Lae, New Guinea and headed for a small speck over two thousand miles away in the vast Pacific Ocean called Howland Island. Her twin-engine Lockheed Electra never reached landfall. The U.S. Navy and Coast Guard went all out to locate Amelia and her navigator, Fred Noonan, but no trace of them was ever found.

Coincidentally, in November 1937, my father resigned from his job at TWA and returned to Southern California to take a position with Lockheed Aircraft Corp. in Burbank. He was supervisor of engine installation on Lockheed Electra aircraft—the same type of aircraft Amelia Earhart was flying on her failed around-the-world flight.

My father had fifteen men working for him and his salary was 66 cents per hour. He and his crew installed the complete engine assembly, firewalls, cowling, props, tail pipes, heater tubes, exhaust analyzers, plumbing, controls, and electrical connections. He worked on Lockheed's all-metal ships, including the Electra and Army versions of the Electra, the C-40 and C-40A. He also performed various tasks throughout the final assembly and flight service departments.

Besides the dark incidents occurring in 1937, there were some positive events as well. On May 27th the Golden Gate Bridge opened in San Francisco. During a time of grave economic crisis the iconic international-orange span loomed as a symbol of American spirit and ingenuity, spanning the imposing entrance to San Francisco Bay. Opening day of the bridge was specified "Pedestrian Day" with approximately 200,000 persons trekking across the 4,200-foot-long suspension bridge. I would learn later in life that my future stepmother was one of those multitudes.

The first jet engine prototypes were built and tested on the ground during these years, hinting at the future of aviation but unimaginable to most. A radar system was demonstrated by the U.S. Army Signal Corps to the War Department (now called the Department of Defense). A crude and short-range device at the time, the needs of a world war escalated its development exponentially. Across the Atlantic the British were further ahead in the development of this capability. They called it RDF for Range and Direction Finding.

Several significant aircraft types emerged in 1937. Boeing devoted the year to the production of large, four-engine aircraft, among them the YB-17 bomber (prototype version of the B-17). Lockheed Aircraft designed a new pursuit aircraft for the Army designated the P-38 Lightning which would become a famous WWII fighter. Piper Aircraft Corp began producing the popular Piper J-3 Cub. Taylor-Young Airplane Co. began building the Taylorcraft, competitor to the Piper Cub, and Douglas Aircraft continued building the much sought after DC-3.

The clouds of war began descending once again over Europe in 1938. In March, German troops seized Austria on the pretext they were protecting pro-German Austrians suffering violent persecution. In a meeting in Munich in September, France and England in essence gave the Sudetenland in Czechoslovakia away to Germany. Although the Czechs weren't even part of the negotiations, they had to endure German troops entering their land the very next day. The word "Munich" became a synonym for "disastrous appeasement."

President Roosevelt signed a bill creating the U.S. Civil Aeronautics Authority (CAA) in 1938. With its establishment, civilian air transportation came under federal control. In September, my father's Post Commander from his Army days at March Field was promoted to Chief of the Army Air Corps—but by then Henry "Hap" Arnold was a Brigadier General.

That year Howard Hughes circled the earth in a Lockheed 14 monoplane in just over three and one-half days—a record. The attention the plane received from the flight resulted in both commercial and military overseas orders for Lockheed. Imperial Airways of London ordered a "fleet" of the planes and the British Air Ministry (BAM) ordered 250 of the military version called the Hudson bomber. Australia ordered another 50 of the bomber version. My father was still working for Lockheed and in November was promoted to a lead position with six junior assemblymen working under him.

Other significant events occurring in 1938 included the discovery of nuclear fission. A British engineer demonstrated color television in London and the Douglas Aircraft Company began producing the DC-4. This four-engine successor to the DC-3 carried 42 passengers and had an innovative tricycle landing gear.

It was also the year of "Wrong Way Corrigan." Forbidden to fly solo across the Atlantic Ocean in his nine-year-old Curtiss Robin, Douglas G. Corrigan filed a flight plan for a flight from New York to California. When he actually ended up landing in

Ireland, he said he had gotten confused and flown the wrong way. The Bureau of Air Commerce suspended his experimental license, afraid he would attempt to make the hazardous return trip back to New York.

In 1939, the world changed dramatically. The year started out similarly to previous years, but uncontrollable events began to change the way of life for the people of the United States and the world. Except for the Japanese incursion into China, the world was generally at peace at the beginning of the year. The Spanish Civil War had ended on April 1 after three years of bloody conflict.

The World's Fair opened in New York with a "World of Tomorrow" theme. The fair featured new technology, such as the public debut of television, and an upbeat vision of the future. Hollywood outdid itself with new films in 1939. Both *Gone with the Wind* and *The Wizard of Oz* opened, as well as *Mr. Smith Goes to Washington* with Jimmy Stewart and *Stagecoach* with John Wayne.

America was largely rural in 1939. In fact, until the 1920s, more people lived in the countryside than in cities. The United States was just beginning to recover from the depths of the Great Depression. People counted their pennies and rejoiced in the simple pleasures of life. With the exception of the few major cities which existed at the time, Americans were leading a rather quiet and slow-paced life.

This is the life into which I was born at Fair Oaks Hospital on Fair Oaks Avenue in Pasadena, California on February 1, 1939. My parents finally had a child, but because I was born by Caesarean section, they decided to forego having any more children. My 20-year-old mother had not been in the best of health throughout her short life and neither she nor my father wanted her to have to go through another possible C-section.

Sometime after my birth my parents moved to the San Fernando Valley, living at 10972-½ Ratner Street in Roscoe.

Today Roscoe is no longer a city, the only remnant of it being a street bearing that name. Nineteen thirty-nine was the year Nazi Germany tested the world's first jet aircraft and, ominously, signed a military alliance known as the "Pact of Steel" with Fascist Italy.

At dawn on September 1, 1939, Hitler's Army stormed into Poland with such force and at such speed that a new phrase was added to the world's vocabulary: "Blitzkrieg" or "Lightning War." France and Great Britain quickly declared war on Germany. Making matters worse, the Soviet Union invaded Finland. These actions, along with the Japanese rampage in China, were the first acts of a second world war.

At that time, the United States was considered to be a fifth- or sixth-rate air power by the Chief of the General Headquarters Air Force of the U.S. Army. As it was at the beginning of World War I, America found itself with a lot of catching up to do.

In the world of American aviation, things began to change rapidly, however. Overseas orders for aircraft, as well as those from the U.S. Army and Navy, quickly picked up in 1939. The aircraft industry reached it highest level of activity in its thirty-year history. Notable, among others, was Boeing Airplane Company's 49 B-17A Flying Fortress, built for the Army Air Corps. Consolidated Aircraft Corp. secured the largest single aircraft purchase in U.S. Naval history with an order for a fleet of PBY-5A amphibian aircraft.

Fairchild Aviation Corp. began producing the PT-19 trainer and Boeing's Wichita Division started building the Stearman PT-13A primary trainer, both for the U.S. Army Air Corps. My father was to fly both types, but at the time, was still working at Lockheed, which was producing large quantities of Hudson bombers for the BAM.

My father had not logged any flight time for three years. He finally took to the air again in a Taylor J-2 Cub. And in an action that would directly affect my father's flying future, President Roosevelt signed the Civilian Pilot Training Act on June 27, 1939. This act empowered the Civil Aeronautics Authority (CAA) to establish the Civilian Pilot Training Service (CPT) with the purpose of training 95,000 civilian pilots over the next five-year period. My father would become one of them.

In 1940, German troops stormed across Europe aided by tanks (Panzers), motorized artillery, and coordinated air strikes from the German Air Force's (Luftwaffe) dreaded, screeching Stuka dive-bombers. Denmark and Norway fell to the Nazi forces. Next the Netherlands, Belgium, Luxembourg, and then Northern France succumbed. The Nazi Swastika flew over Paris. As was the fate of the other Nazi-occupied cities in Europe, freedom's flame had been extinguished in the City of Light. These events would inspire the popular song "When the Lights Go on Again (All Over the World)." It was a tragic time for Europe and the free world.

As the Germans closed in on France, the British Expeditionary Forces and some French troops were successfully evacuated from the beaches of Dunkirk. Superhuman effort and every ship that could float, no matter its size, were brought to bear to extract the forces of freedom from the beaches. Great Britain now stood alone against Nazi tyranny.

Beginning with a directive from Adolph Hitler in July 1940 and climaxing in September of that year, the Luftwaffe attempted to subdue England by air superiority alone. In what would become known as the "Battle of Britain," dense formations of Heinkel, Dornier, and Junkers bombers, escorted by Messerschmitt 109 and 110 fighters, ran a gauntlet of barrage balloons, anti-aircraft guns, and Royal Air Force (RAF) Spitfires and Hurricanes to bomb London. The British, who called it "the Blitz," outlasted Germany, thanks in large part to the use of the British-developed RDF stations and the brave pilots of the RAF. Great Britain's new Prime Minister, Winston Churchill, said of these aviators, "Never in the field of human conflict was so much owed by so many to so few."

Mercedes with new son, Ken Jr. (1939)

Left to right: Kenneth & Mercedes Chastain, Thelma & Dewitt Pyeatt

Mercedes boarding a TWA DC-2 bound for Kansas City, Missouri (1936).

Mercedes in the cockpit of a Fairchild FC-2 – Winslow, Arizona (1937)

Chapter 5
War Comes to America

He inspected the machines of war
The Japanese bombed Pearl
His parents, in the line of fire,
Watched the War unfurl

As war exploded throughout Europe, American leadership realized a pressing need for a buildup of U.S. Armed Forces. The Selective Training and Service Act was approved by Congress in September 1940. This Act required all males between the ages of 21 and 35 to register with their local Draft Board. At age 27, my father had already served three years in the Army and was married with a child, so he didn't have to worry about being drafted.

President Roosevelt was re-elected for an unprecedented third term in 1940. In May he asked Congress to pass legislation to make it possible to increase the aircraft industry's production capacity to 50,000 airplanes per year. The Army and the Navy agreed to give France (while she was still in the war) and Britain virtually unhindered access to the latest models of American warplanes. America had become "the Arsenal of Democracy."

In September, the War Department notified American airplane manufacturers to "tool up" in preparation for mass production orders. There were many contributors to the war effort in the field of aviation, among them Boeing, who built 53 B-17 bombers. Consolidated Aircraft Corp. in San Diego, California, besides building PBY Catalina flying boats for the Navy, built six B-24 Liberator bombers for the Army Air Corps.

Douglas Aircraft Co. received the largest military order ever placed with one company in America and began construction on a $20 million aircraft plant in Long Beach, California. Besides building more of its commercial DC-3 transports, Douglas built military versions of it. In addition, Douglas built the Dauntless dive-bomber, along with other types of military aircraft.

Fairchild Aircraft built PT-19 and PT-26 primary trainers, among others, for the military. Even the automobile industry got into the act. Ford Motor Co. began building aircraft engines and General Motors started manufacturing airplane propellers.

Lockheed Aircraft Corp. produced more Hudson bomber variants and P-38 Lightning fighters, as well as several versions of the Lodestar transport aircraft. Glen Martin Co. developed a new twin-engine bomber designated the B-26 Marauder, and North American built the AT-6 Texan advanced trainer.

In October my father left Lockheed Aircraft to take the position of Senior Inspector in the Procurement Division of the United States Army Air Corps (USAAC) at Vultee Field in Downey, California. The family moved to 449 Cabell Street in Bellflower, California to be closer to his new job.

In the area of commercial aviation, Piper Aircraft built over 3,000 Piper Cubs that year. Stinson Aircraft Division was taken over by Vultee Aircraft and continued production of its three-place Stinson Voyager. Meanwhile, Vultee Aircraft itself was busy building BT-13 and BT-15 Valiant basic trainers, as well as P-66 Vanguard fighters with my father overseeing production as a government inspector.

In 1941, events took even more tragic twists and turns, beginning on June 22. In an operation named "Barbarossa," German troops invaded the Soviet Union. In only six weeks, there were German Panzer Divisions within 220 miles of Moscow. With the increasing aggressiveness of Japan in the late 1930s and the outbreak of full-scale war in Europe, the U.S. Navy made efforts to expand and improve the Naval Base at Pearl Harbor, Hawaiian Territory.

A decision was made to hold the U.S. Pacific Fleet's exercises off Hawaii in 1940. After completion of maneuvers the Pacific Fleet remained at Pearl Harbor. In February 1941, the fleet's permanent base was switched from San Diego to Hawaii. With this shift, expansion of the Pearl Harbor Naval Base was begun to accommodate the entire U.S. Pacific Fleet.

Volunteering for this grand enterprise, my father's parents found themselves headed for Oahu, Hawaii. A skilled carpenter, Everett began working construction on Pearl Harbor's Ford Island. Ann and Everett settled in at 296F South Vineyard in Honolulu.

In June, the Army Air Corps organized a Ferry Command, whose function was to fly airplanes manufactured in the United States across the ocean for delivery to the British. That same month the U.S. War Department reorganized the U.S. Army Air Corps, integrating its air activities and changing its name to the U. S. Army Air Forces.

Up to that point in the buildup of arms, domestic airlines in the United States had to sacrifice 125 transport planes to the British war effort. In October, the Army Air Forces announced the delivery and flight-testing of the first twin-engine Beech AT-11 Kansan meant for bombing and gunnery training. My father was to obtain his instrument rating in an AT11A modified as a navigation trainer.

On December 7, 1941, there were two United States Naval task forces (TF) at sea in the Pacific. One TF was formed around the aircraft carrier USS *Lexington* (CV-2). It was on a course for Midway, ferrying Vought SB2U-3 Vindicators to a Marine scout bombing squadron there. The second TF was formed around the aircraft carrier USS *Enterprise* (CV-6). It was returning from a covert mission delivering Marine F4F-3 Wildcat fighters to Wake Island and still at sea. Thus, when the Japanese Navy suddenly attacked the U.S. military bases on Oahu, America's carriers with their onboard aircraft were safely at sea.

The third aircraft carrier of the U.S. Pacific Fleet was the USS *Saratoga* (CV-3). Having just completed an overhaul in Bremerton, Washington it was tied up at NAS San Diego, North Island on December 7. She was readying to get underway with her own air group, a Marine air squadron and miscellaneous aircraft being ferried to Pearl Harbor. These too were safe from harm.

Hawaiian land-based aircraft weren't so lucky. As a result of the attack, the majority of Army Air Corps planes at Hickam, Bellows, and Wheeler Fields were either damaged or destroyed. The Navy air bases at Ford Island and Kaneohe Bay along with the Marine airfield at Ewa were also hit resulting in heavy aircraft loss and damage.

The attack on the U.S. Naval Base at Pearl Harbor cost the Navy heavily. Twenty-one ships of the U.S. Pacific Fleet were either sunk or damaged, including six battleships. 2,400 soldiers, sailors and civilians were killed. President Roosevelt declared to the nation that December 7 was a day that would "live in infamy." The United States was at war with Japan. Four days later Hitler declared war on the United States.

Ann and Everett were in Honolulu when the attack took place. On December 9, Everett sent a telegram to his adult children that simply said, "=SAFE=, =EVERETT CHASTAIN=." On December 23, Ann wrote a letter back home describing their experiences during the raid. What follows are excerpts from that letter:

WELL DARLINGS, I WILL TRY TO WRITE YOU SOME OF THE NEWS. FIRST I WANT TO SAY THAT WE ARE BOTH WELL AND GETTING ALONG FINE AND HOPE THAT ALL OF YOU THERE ARE THE SAME . . . PLEASE LET ALL THE REST READ THIS FOR I WILL TRY TO TELL YOU WHAT WE REALLY SAW.

WELL, TO BEGIN WITH WE WENT TO LAU YU CHI'S SAT. NIGHT DECEMBER 6TH. THERE WERE 10 OF US . . . WE HAD A TABLE BY THE DANCE FLOOR AND OUR DINNER WAS GRAND. I GUESS IT WILL BE THE LAST ONE TOO FOR A LONG TIME . . . WE GOT HOME AROUND MIDNIGHT AS WE WEREN'T IN ANY HURRY, FOR DAD WASN'T GOING TO WORK THE NEXT DAY. WE HAD PLANNED WITH THE ANGELOS TO GO ON A PICNIC AROUND THE ISLAND AND TAKE SOME MORE PICTURES. WE WOKE UP AROUND 7:30 A.M. AND I STARTED BREAKFAST. I WAS GOING TO MAKE BISCUITS AND HAVE A REAL NICE BREAKFAST, BUT, OH BOY! HOW IT TURNED OUT. WE HEARD THE NOISE BUT THOUGHT IT WAS A PRACTICE DRILL AND I KEPT ON GETTING THE BREAKFAST. PRETTY SOON LORETTA CAME TO THE DOOR AND SAID, 'ANN HAVE YOU GOT YOUR RADIO ON?' SHE WAS CRYING. WE QUICKLY TURNED IT ON AND THE ANNOUNCER WAS SAYING 'LADIES AND GENTLEMEN, THIS IS A REAL ATTACK BY THE JAPANESE.' WE COULDN'T BELIEVE IT.

WE WENT OUTSIDE AND LOOKED UP IN THE AIR. AT FIRST WE COULDN'T SEE A THING BUT THE BURSTING OF ANTI-AIRCRAFT SHELLING FROM OUR OWN GUNS. WE COULD SEE THE SMOKE FROM PEARL HARBOR AND THE NOISE IN THE AIR WAS AWFUL. THEN WE SAW SOME PLANES FLY RIGHT OVER OUR HOUSE. WE COUNTED 15 IN FORMATION AND HERE'S THE FUNNY PART OF IT ALL. DAD DIDN'T HAVE HIS GLASSES BUT HE COULD SEE THE RISING SUN ON THE WINGS.

WE NEVER THOUGHT ABOUT IT AT THE TIME BUT LATER ON I TOLD HIM HE DIDN'T NEED GLASSES TO SEE OR FIND ANYTHING. IN THE MEANTIME VINCE HAD DRESSED AND LEFT FOR DUTY, AND THE RADIO WAS CALLING FOR DIFFERENT WORKMEN TO GO TO THEIR JOBS AND FOR OTHERS TO STAND BY. DAD'S DEPARTMENT WASN'T CALLED BUT HE WENT TO WORK MONDAY AROUND 9:00 A.M. AND WAS SENT TO PEARL HARBOR TO WORK AND HE HAS BEEN THERE EVER SINCE.

WHEN THESE PLANES FLEW OVER, WE SAW THEM DIVING OVER THE HARBOR AND ABOUT THAT TIME WE HEARD AN AWFUL NOISE WHICH SEEMED RIGHT ON US AND WE DIDN'T KNOW WHAT IT WAS. BUT WHEN WE HEARD THE SECOND NOISE WE DECIDED IT WAS BOMBS, SO WE WENT INTO THE HOUSE AND LAID ON THE FLOOR. THEN WE HEARD ANOTHER ONE. THE FIRST BOMB THAT WE HEARD FELL IN THE GROUNDS OF OUR GOVERNOR ABOUT ½ BLOCK FROM US. THE SECOND ONE ABOUT 1½ AND THE THIRD ONE FELL ABOUT 2½ BLOCKS AWAY. I CAN'T TELL YOU HOW IT SOUNDED, ONLY THAT IT WAS A QUEER HISSING SOUND.

WHEN DAD SAW WHAT KIND OF PLANES THEY WERE HE JUST PUT HIS ARM AROUND ME AND SAID, 'LET'S GO IN HONEY' AND WE HAD LORETTA COME IN WITH US TOO. AND STILL WE COULDN'T BELIEVE IT WAS TRUE, ALTHOUGH THE RADIO KEPT SAYING IT WAS THE REAL McCOY. THEY MADE 3 ATTACKS ON US, BUT THANK GOD THEY DIDN'T ACCOMPLISH WHAT THEY WANTED TO DO. IT LASTED ABOUT 1½ HOURS AND AT ½ HOUR INTERVALS. THEY WERE FLYING THEIR PLANES VERY LOW ON THE HIGHWAY AND MACHINE GUNNING THE CARS THAT WERE CARRYING THE MEN TO WORK; ALSO, FLYING OVER THE HOUSES WITH THEIR MACHINE GUNS BLASTING AWAY. AT 5:15 MONDAY MORNING ONE WENT RIGHT DOWN VINEYARD, BUT I UNDERSTAND IT WAS ONE OF OUR OWN. I GUESS IT WAS TO LET THE JAPS HERE ON THE ISLAND KNOW WE COULD DO IT TOO AND THEY BETTER LOOK OUT AND NOT START ANYTHING ON THE ISLAND.

WE ARE HAVING BLACK OUT EVERY NIGHT. THE FIRST NIGHT OF BLACK OUT THEY SHOT OUT 42 LIGHTS. IF THEY SEE A LIGHT ON THEY HOLLER 'TURN OUT YOUR LIGHTS' AND IF THEY DON'T DO IT—WHAM!—OUT GOES YOUR LIGHT ANYWAY. NO ONE ELSE IS ALLOWED ON THE STREETS AFTER DARK UNLESS IT IS ABSOLUTELY NECESSARY AND YOU MUST PROVE YOURSELF AND YOUR REASON FOR BEING ON THE STREET. WE HAD OUR BATHROOM AND KITCHEN BLACKED OUT WITH BLACK CLOTH OVER THE WINDOWS AND LIGHTS AND OUR LIGHT IN THE ICEBOX IS BLACKED OUT TOO. WE GO TO BED REAL EARLY AND LISTEN TO THE RADIO. IT WAS OFF THE AIR AS FAR AS PROGRAMMING WAS CONCERNED TILL THE 13TH. WE WERE ASKED TO KEEP OUR RADIOS ON JUST THE SAME SO THEY COULD TELL US THE NEWS AT DIFFERENT TIMES. DAD AND I ARE GETTING LOTS OF REST OUT OF IT ANYWAY.

WE HAD AN AIR RAID ALARM THAT LASTED 33 MINUTES LAST SUNDAY. ALSO, SOME PRACTICE ALARMS, BUT THEY ARE ALL REAL TO ME. WE ARE 'DIGGING IN' HERE NOW AND MAKING BOMB SHELTERS. I HOPE WE NEVER HAVE TO USE THEM. THE TOWN IS SO DIFFERENT NOW WITH ALL THE BARRICADES AND MACHINE GUN NESTS AT ALL THE IMPORTANT PLACES. SOME OF THE WOMEN ARE BEING EVACUATED AND I MAY BE LATER ON. I DON'T KNOW YET, OF COURSE . . . I SURE HOPE DAD CAN COME WITH ME. BUT IF HE CAN'T, I WILL HAVE TO MAKE THAT SACRIFICE OF LEAVING HIM AS EVERYONE WILL HAVE TO SACRIFICE SOMETHING TO WIN THIS WAR.

WELL DARLINGS, I HOPE YOU WILL KNOW HOW WE FELT OVER YOU KIDS WHEN WE WERE BEING ATTACKED, AND I SENT YOU THE WIRE AS SOON AS I COULD GET NERVE TO GO DOWNTOWN. I JUST COULDN'T SEEM TO THINK, I WAS SO STUNNED OVER IT ALL DAY MONDAY FOLLOWING. THAT IS WHY I DIDN'T SEND WORD SOONER . . .

LOVING MOTHER AND DAD

After December 7, Everett went to work on Ford Island rebuilding what the Japanese had destroyed. It wasn't long before Ann was required to return to the U.S. mainland where she volunteered for the Communication Corps watching out for enemy aircraft.

On December 13, 1941, President Roosevelt had issued a proclamation placing the War Department in complete control of civil aviation. Soon afterward all civilian flying was banned along the West Coast.

Ann Chastain in her Communication Corps. uniform. The Communication Corps. acted as coastal aircraft spotters, watching out for enemy aircraft. Civilian flying was not allowed near the West Coast after the Japanese attack on Pearl Harbor.

Chapter 6
"Equality of Sacrifice"

Putting normal lives on hold
The people donned the yoke
To fight the common enemy
And the sleeping giant woke

My father was still working as an inspector when the war broke out. The Factory Resident Representative, Colonel L.C. Johnson, soon took him off of inspection and made him Assistant Chief Inspector and also placed him in charge of the entire office force. In his new capacity, his yearly salary was $2,600. In compliance with President Roosevelt's December 13th proclamation, the War Department now had complete control of civil aviation.

In 1941, Aeronca Aircraft Corp. started producing large quantities of L-3 Defenders for the Army Air Forces. Piper Aircraft Corp. delivered forty-four L-4 Grasshoppers and Taylor Aircraft Corp. delivered twenty-four L-2 Grasshoppers. The Army used these small airplanes as spotter aircraft, among other duties.

Boeing Airplane Company produced 144 B-17 Flying Fortresses in Seattle. In Wichita, Boeing was building PT-13 and

PT-17 Kaydet primary trainers for the Army and Navy. The company had acquired the Stearman Aircraft Company of Wichita, Kansas in 1934, which became a Boeing subsidiary. In 1939, the Stearman subsidiary became the Boeing Division of Wichita. In less than a year, my father flew both the PT-13 and PT-17.

At Vultee Aircraft, Inc. where my father was working as Assistant Chief Inspector, they were busy building over 1,800 BT-13 and SNV Valiant trainers for the Army and Navy, respectively. Additionally, Vultee was manufacturing more than seventy P-66 Vanguard pursuit planes, mainly for China.

Waco Aircraft Corp. was manufacturing over 600 of its UPF-7 commercial biplane. This model was adopted for wide use in the government's Civilian Pilot Training (CPT) program. Although fourteen of the military version, designated YPT-14, were built, it was not adopted for operational use. Later my father would fly the Waco UPF-7 when attending CPT secondary school in Prescott, Arizona.

In 1942, Germany and Japan were running rampant in each of their spheres of conquest. At the same time, America was getting into high gear to fight the war. Prices were fixed and gasoline, rubber, sugar, meat, and other items were rationed. This "equality of sacrifice" as President Roosevelt phrased it, helped to redirect the economy toward the production of airplanes, tanks, and other equipment of war. Also, the production of new cars in the U.S. was banned and would remain so until 1945.

The war affected every single person in the country and my parents were no exception. Up until rationing went into effect, they both used sugar in their coffee, but because of rationing, restaurant waitstaff put it in. They added too much for my parent's taste, so they stopped requesting sugar altogether, never to use it again. "War Time" went into effect, moving all U.S. clocks ahead one hour. Priorities were set for civilian travel on domestic airlines and my father took a military furlough from his Assistant Chief Inspector position to enlist in the Army Reserve Corps.

In July he left Southern California to attend Civilian Pilot Training (CPT) primary school. He spent August through September flying a J-3 Cub at James Flying Service in Prescott, Arizona. He had to go to Arizona to attend flight school because civilian flying was restricted along the coast due to the threat of Japanese invasion.

Invasion was a real and frightening threat to the people of the West Coast for good reason. From December 18 to December 24, 1941, nine Japanese submarines positioned at strategic points along the U.S. West Coast attacked eight American merchant ships. Two ships were sunk, two were damaged and six seamen were killed. On February 23, 1942, the Japanese Submarine I-17 shelled the Ellwood Oil Company refinery just ten miles north of Santa Barbara, California and in June, a Japanese submarine shelled the Oregon coast.

After completing primary training, my father attended CPT secondary training at James Flying Service. CPT training came into existence as a result of a bill signed by President Roosevelt in 1939 to train 95,000 civilian pilots. As one of that number, my father found himself flying a Waco UPF-7 from October to November.

In April 1942, the United States struck a blow at Japan when Lt. Colonel "Jimmy" Doolittle and his squadron of sixteen B-25 Mitchell medium bombers carried out the first bombing mission against Tokyo from the aircraft carrier USS *Hornet* (CV-8). When asked where these Army bombers flew from, President Roosevelt responded, "Shangri-La," referring to the imaginary, hidden utopia described in the novel *Lost Horizon* by the English author James Hilton.

Men weren't the only gender responding to the war effort. The Women's Army Auxiliary Corps (WAACs) was created in

May. This organization gave women the opportunity to serve with the Army. They worked as telephone operators, drivers, airplane spotters, secretaries, etc. More than 13,000 women applied on the first day of registration. Women also joined the Navy Auxiliary (WAVEs) and the Women Air Force Service Pilots (WASP).

The Manhattan Project was conceived in 1942. The race was on to beat Germany in splitting the atom and releasing the destructive force of atomic energy. In December a major step in that direction was taken when American physicist Enrico Fermi achieved the first sustained nuclear chain reaction.

On October 1, America's first jet plane, Bell Aircraft's XP-59A Airacomet, took off on its initial flight from Muroc Army Air Field in California—today's Edwards Air Force Base. The plane's performance was found to be unsatisfactory and compared unfavorably to the propeller-driven North American P-51 Mustang. It never saw combat. Nevertheless, America had taken its first step toward the jet-propelled future of aviation.

In November 1942, my father reported to the 1st Army Air Forces Flying Training Detachment at Hancock College of Aeronautics in Santa Maria, California. He had taken a civilian position there as a flight instructor. After obtaining his Certificate of Proficiency, he began teaching Army cadets the primary phase of flying in 225-HP Lycoming-powered Stearman PT-13s.

Hancock College was one of the original eight experienced civilian flying schools the Chief of the Army Air Forces, General Henry "Hap" Arnold, called upon in 1939 to begin training Army Air Forces cadets in the primary phase of flying. Hancock College and the rest of the civilian flight school system became an integral part of the Air Force's training program. These programs freed up Army pilots for combat flying rather than having them assigned as instructors. It was the civilian flight instructors who prepared new Army cadets in the craft of flying.

In 1943, the balance of power began a worldwide shift for the Allied Forces. In the Pacific, U.S. Marines landed on Guadalcanal, beginning the first major U.S. amphibious operation in the Pacific. The Americans were now on the offensive. In the North Atlantic, the Allies attained the ability to limit their losses from German U-boat attacks through better detection methods and improved air coverage. It was finally possible to produce more tonnage in ships than was lost to sinking. Meanwhile, the Allies drove the Germans out of North Africa and invaded Italy.

After successfully leading the North African campaign, "Operation Torch," General Dwight D. Eisenhower was named Supreme Commander of Allied Forces for the invasion of the European mainland. In October, the U.S. Air Transport Command (ATC) inaugurated its aerial freight delivery service between Patterson Field, Ohio and Assam, India—a distance of 14,000 miles.

My father continued training Army cadets in 1943, mostly flying PT-13s, but also flying PT-17s and BT-15s. The PT-17 was just like the PT-13 except it had a 225-HP Continental engine. Both primary trainers had a top speed of 120 mph. The Vultee BT-15 Valiant basic trainer was powered with a 450-HP Wright engine. It also had retractable landing gear, which, along with its more powerful engine, gave it a top speed of 185 mph.

Meanwhile, the United States was outdoing itself in producing military aircraft. Well over 85,000 airplanes of all types were produced for the U.S. Armed Forces in 1943. In a giant leap forward, the Boeing Airplane Company, in addition to its B-17 Flying Fortresses and BT-13 Kaydet trainers my father was flying, began producing the B-29 Superfortress. The B-29 was the single greatest airplane program undertaken during World War II.

In January 1944, my mother and I joined my father in Santa Maria and moved into a house at 813 East Cook Street. While living there, I played with several of the neighborhood kids who also had fathers stationed at Hancock College of Aeronautics. One day while we were playing, I came up with the idea of walking to the airfield. Near our houses was a large agricultural field that ran all the way to Hancock College. Several of us children took off walking down the field with the intention of visiting our fathers. We walked and walked and walked some more. As we went farther and farther kids started dropping out and heading back home. I stuck with it, however, and was the only one to make it all the way to the base's main gate.

When I arrived, I proudly presented myself to the guard and asked to see my father. He made a phone call and I waited. I never did see my father that day. Of course, he was busy with the war effort and couldn't be distracted. I'm not sure, but I believe my mother was summoned to come and take me home. I don't remember being punished for that escapade—after all, I was just a loving son trying to see his father.

In the United States, communal plots and backyard patches became what were known as "victory gardens." By tending these gardens, Americans addressed the scarcity of vegetables and promoted a sense of pride in being able to contribute to the war effort, if only in a small way. I remember our victory garden in the backyard of our Santa Maria home very clearly. Although I was too young to help in any significant way, I remember my father working on the garden and felt the family pride resulting from it.

President Roosevelt won his fourth term as President in 1944. This was also the year the Second World War came to its climax. In the Pacific, U.S. forces returned to the Philippines at Leyte. The Russians made relentless, though costly, advances against the German armies in the east. In the south, Italy was liberated in May. The Royal Air Force Bomber Command's night raids, paired with the U.S. Eighth Air Force's precision daylight raids, strangled German war production—and the P-51 Mustang was introduced to the European

Theatre of Operations, providing the range necessary for fighter escort all the way to Berlin. Allied air attacks on German cities and industry became merciless.

In March, my father left his instructor position at Hancock College and entered the U.S. Army Air Transport Pilot Training School (ATPT) at Deming Army Air Field in Deming, New Mexico. At Deming he received instrument training in BT-13 Valiant basic trainers. According to my father, the BT-13 was sarcastically known as the Vultee Vibrator because it would really shake when close to a stall. He also flew his first dual engine aircraft, the Beechcraft AT-11A advanced trainer on April 30, 1944. Flying it, he received his Instrument Flying Certificate.

My father was in Class 44-3 DAAF (Deming Army Air Field). His class book shows a picture of him looking very smart in his flight jacket, military cap and earphones. The caption under the picture states: "Flight Leader, A-Flight, Squadron 3." The book also contains several pages of family photos. It is filled with the pictures of wives, girlfriends, and children. One of the pictures is of me, a five-year-old towhead. The caption under my picture reads, "Old man Chastain's boy, 'Ken.'" At 30 years of age, my father was considered to be "Old man Chastain."

On D-Day, June 6, 1944, in "Operation Overlord," 155,000 Allied troops invaded German-occupied France. In what was the defining moment of the war in Europe, thousands of brave young men either landed on the beaches of Normandy or parachuted behind enemy lines. Wave after wave of landing craft reached the beaches as a gigantic sky train, nine planes wide and 200 miles long, carried American and British airborne troops across the English Channel. By nightfall of the first day, more than 3,000 fathers, sons and brothers had sacrificed their lives for their country.

Just nine days after D-Day, a group of B-29 Superfortresses dropped the first bombs on the Japanese mainland since General Doolittle led his daring, but token, raid on Tokyo in 1942.

U.S. Army Air Transport Pilot Training School (ATPT)
Deming, New Mexico. Kenneth L. Chastain, Flight Leader,
A-Flight, Squadron 3 (Class 44-3 DAAF)

Kenneth at Civilian Pilot Training (CPT) school, James Flying Service, Prescott, Arizona (1942)

Ken Jr. playing war with Grandfather Aaron Dewitt Pyeatt (Poppy)

Mr. & Mrs. Kenneth L. Chastain and son; Kenneth with Hancock Field flight jacket and Ken Jr. in a precursor uniform

Mercedes and Ken Jr. leave for Santa Maria (January 1943)

Kenneth in his Hancock College of Aeronautics uniform (1942)

Hot Stearman PT-13 pilot Kenneth Chastain (1943)

Kenneth in the cockpit of a Vultee BT-15 Valiant (1943)

Hancock College class photo. Kenneth is the instructor in the middle (1944).

Chapter 7
Flight Officer – Service Pilot

She worked in the Douglas factory
He ferried planes Down Under
Each doing their part for victory
While the Pacific raged like thunder

On June 24, 1944, my father graduated from Air Transport Pilot Training and received his wings. He was commissioned as a Flight Officer-Service Pilot in the Army of the United States on June 27 and was transferred to the Army Air Corps Air Transport Command at Long Beach Army Airfield. He was attached to the 556th AAF Base Unit (6th Ferrying Division, ATC) 28th Ferrying Squadron. Although he was not subject to the draft, he joined the millions of other Americans going off to war.

In April, my mother and I moved to 3729 Sebren Avenue in Long Beach, California in what was then called "Lakewood Village." My parents purchased the house in July. For the first time in their married life, they were homeowners.

At Long Beach my father received transition qualification, or "familiarization training," in a wide variety of aircraft. These included the Vultee BT13, Cessna UC-78, and Beech

AT-11 trainers, the Douglas C-47B and C-54B transports, and the North American B-25J, Boeing B-17G, and Consolidated B-24L bombers. On August 12, 1944, as copilot on a C47B, my father left Long Beach, California for his first ferry flight to Australia. He flew via John Rogers Airport, Hawaii, Christmas Island, Canton Island (part of the Phoenix Island group), Nandi in the Fiji Islands, and Guadalcanal, ending up in Townsville, Australia. Guadalcanal had been in Japanese hands until its complete pacification on January 8, 1943.

I remember clearly when my father took off from Long Beach on that trip because he, my mother and I had gone to a restaurant on or near the airbase and had a nice dinner together. As we entered the restaurant, I remember the subdued lighting and a cocktail piano being played for the patrons. After dinner, my father left us to board his plane and my mother and I drove around the outside of the base to the end of the runway. As my father's plane came to the end of the runway and readied for takeoff, he flashed his flashlight at us, then he took off into the night.

On August 25, 1944, the city of Paris was liberated. As the Free French and American troops entered the city, they were overwhelmed by human waves of deliriously happy Parisians. Kisses abounded. By the end of the year the Allies were knocking on Germany's door.

On September 13, my father was copilot ferrying a North American B-25J to Amberly Field in Brisbane, Australia. This time he flew via Hawaii, Christmas, Canton, Nandi, and Tontouta on New Caledonia Island. Then again on September 27, he was copilot on a B-25J being ferried to Townsville, Australia, via Hawaii, Christmas, Canton, Tarawa, and Guadalcanal. Tarawa had only been taken from the Japanese in February 1944 in a bloody battle fought by the United States Marines.

In late October of 1944, my father was assigned to temporary duty at Rosecrans Field in St. Joseph, Missouri. He was attached to the 561st AAF Base Unit (1st Operational Training Unit) where he received a course in advanced instrument flying in C-47A aircraft. This resulted in a Multi-engine Instrument Card and knowledge that would soon be essential in keeping him alive.

My mother joined my father while he was in Missouri, but I was left behind with neighbors who lived down the street from our Long Beach home. My parents returned to Long Beach in mid-December.

America in the 1940s was a nation of railroad tracks and trains. Railroad stations in small towns and cities were crowded with men in uniform. Their wives and girlfriends gave them a last embrace as the trains departed, taking them to one of many theatres of war throughout the world.

The end of the year also found my father aboard a sleeper-train heading east. He traveled through Kansas City, Missouri and eventually ended up in Nashville, Tennessee at the Air Transport Command Ferrying Division at Nashville Municipal Airport. There he received his overseas orders. He was to go to Myitkyina, Burma, where he would join pilots flying supplies over the Himalayas to the Chinese and American armies there.

By that point in the war an imaginary female factory worker had come to fame in American folklore. Her name was "Rosie the Riveter" and she set rivets in America's aircraft factories and shipyards. Rosie's real-life counterparts numbered in the millions. By 1944, thirty-five percent of American women were in the war industry's workforce. Forty-two percent of the total employees working in West Coast aircraft plants were women. My mother became one of those numbers when she went to work at the Douglas Aircraft Factory in Long Beach. She wasn't a riveter, but she was one of the multitudes of women keeping the "Arsenal of Democracy" turning out war machines.

Nineteen forty-four saw advancement in the development of jet aircraft in the United States. The Army Air Forces' first jet-propelled fighter, the Bell XP-59A Airacomet, had its first flight back in October of 1942, but had turned out to be unsuitable for combat. Only 33 of them were produced in 1944 and none were used in war. Concept work on America's first successful jet fighter, the Lockheed Aircraft Corp. YP-80 Shooting Star, began in 1943. Rush orders for production version XP-80s was handed to Lockheed in February 1944. These were the fastest jet-propelled fighters yet developed for the USAAF, but arrived too late for use in World War II.

At this time I stayed with my grandmother, Cleo Pyeatt (whom I called "Me Ma") at 376 Clela Street in East Los Angeles, California. We still had our house in Long Beach, but my father was away flying for the Army most of the time and my mother was doing her part at Douglas Aircraft, so for the sake of the war effort, once again I was separated from my father and saw less of my mother. My grandfather, Aaron Dewitt Pyeatt, "Poppy," lived there, too. Other members of the family living with my grandmother on Clela Street were great-grandmother Mary Johnston (whom I called "GG" for "Great Grandmother"), Aunt Juanita Collins (a.k.a. Nita Davis), and my cousin, Vickie Lee Collins (a.k.a. Vickie Raschke).

While staying on Clela Street my cousin Vickie and I wandered through the neighborhood and stumbled upon a large fishpond in someone's backyard. Vickie had been told not to get her dress dirty because it had just been ironed. I started throwing rocks into the water, so Vickie tried it, too. I was five or six and she was two or three years old. There was a slope down to the fishpond and as she tried to throw a rock, she slipped and fell into the pond. I quickly pulled her out and we both went home so she could change into some dry clothes.

I waited outside for her to change. After awhile, I began to wonder why it was taking so long. I went in to check on her and found that Me Ma thought Vickie had been playing with the garden hose and gotten her dress soiled as she had been told not to do. She was being punished. After I explained the situation, Vickie was allowed to go back outside and play.

It was also here that another boy on the block constantly picked on me. One day he started harassing me again when I just happened to have a hammer in my hand. I took as much as I could, then without thinking, threw the hammer at him. I clearly remember seeing blood all over the place. It scared me so much I ran home and hid under my mother's dressing table behind the modesty curtain. When my mother found me, she assured me that I hadn't killed the boy, as I had feared.

On January 25, 1945, I endured a tonsillectomy at Fair Oaks Hospital in Pasadena, California—the same hospital where I was born. I remember the operating room as being very large, sort of like a classroom. I saw a table with a lot of knives laid out in order on top of a table covered with a white cloth. I was given ether through a cone over my face.

When I went under the anesthesia, I experienced a true out-of-body experience. I saw myself on a long train trestle elevated over an endless expanse of dark green water. A train was bearing down on me. The train drew near and I watched it pass close by me as if I were suspended in air next to it. That was all. The next thing I remember was a nurse forcing me to eat something, even though my throat killed me whenever I tried to swallow. I hated that nurse.

In April 1945, I was playing war in a vacant lot next to the house. The lot was full of very high weeds. I pretended I had been shot, fell down, and immediately felt something sting my left leg. I never saw what it was, but I had to get four very large stitches to close the gash in my leg. I have carried that scar, and the memories of Clela Street, with me all of my life. I don't know why these simple incidents have been so indelibly stamped into my brain, possibly because at that age I was just becoming aware of the world around me and because at that time, the world was in complete turmoil.

Many world events reached their climax in the year 1945. On April 12 the United States lost the man who had been its leader for twelve years. America's first president to fly in an airplane and the man who had guided the country through the depths of the Great Depression and the darkest days of World War II was dead. President Franklin Delano Roosevelt died from a cerebral hemorrhage at the age of 63 and the nation was overwhelmed with grief.

On May 8 the Germans surrendered, both Hitler and Mussolini were dead, and Winston Churchill and the new President of the United States, Harry S. Truman, declared V-E Day (Victory-in-Europe); however, the war with the Japanese was still raging. While the major battles were being fought by Allied forces in the Pacific, the Chinese were also battling the Japanese and tying up a million and a half Japanese soldiers who otherwise would have been available to fight Allied troops elsewhere.

Kenneth with his brother, Russ, Russ's wife, Lois, and his son, Ken Jr. (late 1943)

The Chastain siblings, from left to right: Evelyn, Russell, Kenneth, and Neita (late 1943)

Kenneth and Ken Jr. in front of 376 Clela Street East Los Angeles, California, just prior to Kenneth leaving for Burma (1944)

Left to right: Kenneth (USAAF), Mercedes, Dewitt Pyeatt (Douglas Aircraft), Thelma Pyeatt, Chuck Collins (USMC) and Nita Collins (Mercedes' sister and brother-in-law); Clela Street, East Los Angeles, California (1944)

Mr. & Mrs. Kenneth L. Chastain, Clela Street (1944)

Chapter 8
CBI

With granite walls within the clouds
The Rock Pile loomed as if in dare
Still he flew his weary craft
Between its peaks in silent prayer

W ith the Burma Road closed and the Japanese controlling its ports, the only way open to supply the military needs for the entire country of China was by air over the Himalayan Mountains. This treacherous route became known as the "Hump." Considered the most hazardous of all aerial routes, its jagged peaks reached 20,000 feet into the sky. Solid cloud cover and 100-mile-an-hour gales forced pilots to fly far off course, only to crash on snowy peaks or into jungles so dense they hid all traces of plane and crew.

In the northeastern part of India lies the Assam Valley, the closest point for the Allies to reach China. In this far corner of India, with its monsoon heat and malarial mosquitoes, the India-China Division of the Army Air Transport Command (ATC) carved out a series of air bases for springboards over the Hump. After General Stillwell's Chinese and American troops recaptured the airfield at Myitkyina, Burma, ATC was able to fly to China from there as well.

In mid-January 1945 my father headed to India as one of eleven military passengers on an Army C-46 Commando (#43-47107). Passengers sat facing one another on folding bench seats arranged along the fuselage walls. The twin-engine C-46 was affectionately called "Dumbo" because, in flight, its size and shape reminded many of the Walt Disney character of the same name. The Curtiss C-46 was the largest two-engine plane in the world in 1945. Rushed into production in mid-1942 because of the demand for military transports, it was plagued with more than its share of bugs and gremlins. Because of this, it was sometimes referred to as the "Curtiss Calamity."

With a range of only 1,200 miles, the wide Atlantic Ocean to cross, and with wartime overflight restrictions, "Dumbo" and her passengers were embarking on a dangerous adventure. The first stop was Morrison Field in West Palm Beach, Florida; then it was on to Miami Army Air Field located at the 36th Street Airport in Miami. My father was in the same aircraft all the way to India. The plane was filled with spare parts, empty C-46 wing tanks, and eleven passengers squeezed against the fuselage wall.

From Miami they flew on to Borinquen Field in Puerto Rico. There the crew and passengers had to lay over several days because the C-46's landing gear kept coming down after takeoff. The problem had to be fixed because with the wheels sticking down, the aircraft experienced severe drag, reducing its range. The problem was finally fixed and they took off for Georgetown, British Guiana. After an overnight stay in Georgetown, they flew to Belem, Brazil (pronounced "Bah-lim"). After refueling, they proceeded to Natal, Brazil.

There was about a one-week stay in Natal because of more mechanical problems with the C-46. One problem was that the engines were consuming too much fuel, again reducing the aircraft's range; then, two and one-half hours out on the first attempt at flying across the Atlantic Ocean to Ascension Island on the other side, the left engine started to backfire. They returned to Brazil to have the carburetor repaired. This was the main reason for the extended stay. After repairs the pilots flew fuel consumption tests up and down the coast of Brazil to ensure everything was okay.

Finally, the C-46 took off for a second attempt to reach Ascension Island and this time the flight was successful. After an overnight stay on Ascension Island, it was on to Accra, Gold Coast, for another overnight stay, then to El Fasher in Anglo-Egyptian Sudan (now Sudan). They stopped again in Anglo-Egyptian Sudan, this time in Khartoum. After another overnight stay, the next morning it was discovered the wing tanks on the C-46 were dripping fuel. The fuel in the wing tanks had expanded due to the high temperatures, so the stay was extended a couple of days to let them air out.

They flew on to British-controlled Aden (now part of Yemen), avoiding overflight of the Saudi Arabian Peninsula. There was an overnight stay in the City of Aden, where the Queen of Sheba's baths are located, then it was off to the island of Masira in the Indian Ocean, off the coast of Oman. After an overnight stay there, they flew to Karachi, India (now Pakistan).

My father left the C-46 in Karachi and waited for transportation to Calcutta (now Kolkata), India. After reaching Calcutta's Dum Dum Airport, he was transported via C-47 to Myitkyina, Burma, which had been taken back from the Japanese as recently as mid-1944. In Myitkyina, he was attached to the 1348th AAF Base Unit, India China-Division, ATC.

It was from Myitkyina that my father flew supplies to American and Chinese forces over the Hump. More than 1,300 pilots and crewmembers were lost and over 500 transport planes crashed while attempting to cross the Hump. The weather and the terrain posed as much of a hazard as

Japanese fighter aircraft. There were times he flew without lights in pitch darkness with rain seeping into the cockpit and his knees covered with a raincoat. By this time the C-47s being used had just about been flown into the ground and small holes had developed in their cockpits.

Flying C-47Bs, my father took off from his base in Myitkyina, Burma, at 450 feet above sea level, facing a mountain range directly in front of him that rose to a height of 14,000 feet. He said he had to fly up and down the valley in order to gain enough altitude to cross the first range, then fly over the rest of the "Rock Pile" (aka the Hump) and into China.

On some trips my father had to land in a narrow mountain valley to drop off truck parts and supplies for those working on the Ledo Road. Ledo, in Assam, India, was the railhead of the Bengal-Assam railway. The road was built during this period to supply the Chinese and American forces in China as an alternative to the airlift and the Burma Road which had been severed by the Japanese in 1942. It ran from Ledo, through northern Burma, to Kunming in Yunnan Province, China.

Descending, he would circle in among the steep mountain walls in order to lose enough altitude to land on a short runway. He later related, "We had to land practically at full stall and hope we could make it." A plane fully loaded with supplies made it all the harder. At the end of the runway he would "ground loop" to keep the plane from going into a ditch.

During takeoff, because of the short runway and the thin mountain air at 6,000 feet, he would hold the plane on the ground as long as possible while throttling up to full power. Then, in order to clear a hill that loomed in front of him, he would "chandelle" (make an abrupt climbing turn to the right) so he could use the plane's momentum to gain altitude.

As my father phrased it, "The weather was our biggest enemy." In the monsoon season it would pour buckets—400 to 500 inches of rain a year—and most of it fell over a very few months. Often my father would never see the ground until he landed in China and the navigation instruments of that time were very primitive by today's standards. "It was always a nice relief to break out of the clouds and see the runway there ahead of you," he once told me.

My father made 75 round trips over the Hump between February and August of 1945. His most hair-raising experience with the weather came on one trip when he was copilot. He was flying at 18,000 feet and headed into a thunderstorm when the plane began ascending on its own. He closed the throttles all the way to reverse the uncontrolled gain in altitude, but there was no response from the aircraft. The plane began to climb at a rate of 2,000 to 2,500 feet per minute. At that point my father lowered both the flaps and the landing gear, but the plane kept climbing. As he later explained it, "We were bouncing around. It was rough. I was just hoping we didn't get any baseball-sized hail, like they do sometimes." Finally, at 25,000 feet, the plane stopped climbing and began to descend. It kept descending on its own until its altitude was once again 18,000 feet whereupon my father raised the flaps and landing gear and opened the throttles back up.

My father flew into Chinese cities such as Kunming, Luliang, Naning, and Chengkung, often with 50-gallon drums of gasoline for the airplanes in those places. The cargo he carried during his 75 round trips included Chinese infantrymen from the Chinese 6th Army, who were accompanied by mules, each with a Chinese handler. Bamboo poles were used both fore and aft and across the cabin, which, in effect, made individual stalls for the mules. Once, two C-47s were flown to the overhaul depot in Calcutta. During their overhaul it was discovered that over time mule urine had corroded the control cables in the belly of the plane. It was quite fortunate this problem was discovered in time; otherwise, the cables could have parted in flight.

On one trip over the Rock Pile, my father took a walk to the rear of the plane to check things out. To his horror, he discovered some Chinese soldiers attempting to start a fire on the floor of the plane. They were getting reading to cook rice. Fortunately, he stopped them before they caused any real damage. On another trip a mule stuck its head through one of the plane's windows and they couldn't get it out while in flight. There was concern the plane would have problems landing in this configuration, but they made it down okay. (The mule survived as well.)

On subsequent trips he also carried the American Special Forces Group known as the Mars Task Force. Mars was a long-range penetration force whose mission at the time was to threaten the Burma Road held by the Japanese and allow advancing Allied Forces to reopen this critical supply route to China.

Again, as copilot, my father was flying with aircraft captain Don Lerch on a return trip from Kunming. They kept the C-47 climbing and climbing, trying to get on top of the weather. They reached a point where the aircraft stalled and suddenly did a snap roll onto its back. Very fortunately for my father and the rest of the crew, the plane recovered instantly and there was no cargo onboard.

My father qualified as an aircraft Captain on July 7, 1945. After becoming first pilot, while on a trip out of Myitkyina, he was climbing up to cruising altitude when he had an encounter with St. Elmo's fire. Some of it appeared like white worms crawling across the windshield. He could hear the static getting louder and louder in his earphones until he heard a big boom. Looking out he could see that the propellers appeared to have turned into purple disks. After hearing the boom, he turned the plane around and headed back to Myitkyina where the aircraft was checked for radio and other damage.

On August 6, 1945, the United States dropped the first of two atomic bombs on Japan. On August 14 the Japanese surrendered to the Allied Forces and V-J Day (Victory over Japan) was declared. As a small child living in Los Angeles, I remember hearing sirens, horns, and whistles all blaring away and asked what it was all about. That's how I found out the war was finally over.

Word took a little time to get to all of the battlefronts though, for on August 14 my father and eight others received secret orders (Special Orders Number 217) as follows: "The following named . . . (are assigned to temporary duty) . . . for a period not to exceed 15 days for the purpose of hauling mules and upon completion thereof will return to their proper station."

On my father's last mission into China he flew a shipment of beer to thirsty GIs in Kunming. By that time the city was surrounded by machine guns manned by Chinese Communist troops. The war with Japan had ended in August 1945, and the uneasy truce between the Chinese Nationalists and Chinese Communists had ended.

On September 5, my father received orders relieving him of duty with the ATC and assigning him to the 1352nd AAF Base Unit, ATC Search and Rescue at Mohanbari in India's Assam Valley. At that point he was given Demobilization Category Code 3. This code determined when he could go home.

In Search and Rescue my father mostly flew North American B-25Js looking for downed aircraft; however, he also flew Norseman UC-64s, Douglas C-47s, and Stinson L-5s. The closest he ever came to finding a downed aircraft was once when he was flying a B-25J. While flying among the Himalayan peaks, he saw a silver flash and went in close to see what it was. Because of the terrain he was only able to make out what appeared to be the tail section of a C-46. He had a friend who was missing, Les Lackey, so he volunteered to fly an L-5 in to get a closer look. He had to fly into a canyon in order to get the tail number, which turned out to be different than that of his friend's plane. Dad believed that Les was never found. Other than that incident, as he put it, "We chased more darn, shiny rocks."

On his time off my father would fly a model airplane his friend and brother-in-law, Dewitt Pyeatt, had mailed to him. He lost it one day when he went to the mess hall and left it outside while he ate. When he came back outside, the model plane was gone. He never did find out what happened to it.

Some of the best hunting ground in the world at that time was found in the Assam Valley. American soldiers brought in many fine kills. Elephants, tigers, cheetahs, buffalo, and rhinoceros abounded. Unfortunately, kraits, cobras, and other snakes were also numerous. My father went hunting one day and, when he heard what he thought was a tiger in the bush, he fired and accidentally killed a water buffalo. Later an Indian boy came into the base and asked who had killed his water buffalo. Neither my father, nor anyone else, was about to tell who had done it.

On October 18 my father left Mohanbari to report to Replacement Depot #5 in Calcutta. From there he was sent to Chabua, India where he hitched a ride on a C-54 for Karachi, India (now Pakistan). The C-54 had approximately forty seats along the sides of the fuselage. In Karachi he waited several days for a ship back to the States. He ended up on the MS (Motor Ship) *Torens*, which was manned by a Scandinavian crew. The ship traveled through the Suez Canal to Port Said and into the Mediterranean. It passed Gibraltar going on to the Atlantic where they ran into a storm. They proceeded without incident, however, arriving in New York on December 7, 1945, which was coincidentally the fourth anniversary of the attack on Pearl Harbor.

The *Torens* tied up at Staten Island, New York. My father got off the ship and at first opportunity bought some fresh milk. He told me, "Boy, was it good!" He then went by ferry and bus to Camp Shanks in New York where he and the rest of the transit personnel had a steak dinner.

On December 9 he was sent to the Transcon Center at Camp Kilmer, New Jersey for further travel by air to the 556th AAFBU, Long Beach, California. He caught a C-47 at 3 o'clock on the morning of the 13th. It stopped over in Columbus, Ohio along the way and arrived in Long Beach, California on December 14.

As an overseas returnee, on December 27, 1945 my father was granted 45 days of recuperation, rehabilitation, and recovery leave. He also managed to get a few local hours at the controls of a C-47 out of Long Beach. While still in theatre he received the Air Medal and Oak Leaf Cluster for flying the Hump. Later, the Republic of China gave him the China War Memorial Medal. The Army General Order awarding my father and other crewmen the Air Medal stated, in part:

. . . FOR MERITORIOUS ACHIEVEMENT BY PARTICIPATING IN MORE THAN TWO HUNDRED FIFTY (250) HOURS OF OPERATIONAL FLIGHT IN TRANSPORT AIRCRAFT OVER THE DANGEROUS AND DIFFICULT INDIA-CHINA AIR ROUTES, WHERE EXPOSURE TO ENEMY INTERCEPTION AND ATTACK WAS PROBABLE AND EXPECTED. FLYING AT NIGHT AS WELL AS BY DAY, AT HIGH ALTITUDES OVER IMPASSABLE MOUNTAINOUS TERRAIN THROUGH AREAS CHARACTERIZED BY EXTREMELY TREACHEROUS WEATHER CONDITIONS NECESSITATING LONG PERIODS OF OPERATION ON INSTRUMENTS, OFTEN ENCOUNTERING SEVERE ICING CONDITIONS AND MECHANICAL DIFFICULTIES REQUIRING COURAGEOUS AND SUPERIOR PERFORMANCE OF THEIR RESPECTIVE DUTIES TO OVERCOME, THEY ACCOMPLISHED THEIR MISSIONS WITH DISTINCTION. THEIR ACHIEVEMENT IN THE FACE OF THE HAZARDS AND DIFFICULTIES FACED REGULARLY AND CONTINUOUSLY WITH STEADFAST DEVOTION TO DUTY, REFLECT MUCH CREDIT ON THEMSELVES AND THE ARMY AIR FORCES OF THE UNITED STATES.

I remember the day my father returned to our Lakewood Village home. My mother had left the house and I was staying with my great-grandmother. I kept asking G.G. where my mother was going. I guess I suspected something was up. She finally broke down and told me my mother was going to pick up my father who had just returned from overseas. I was so excited I ran down to the corner to wait for him. I remember my mother being upset with my great-grandmother for two reasons: One, she had spoiled the surprise my mother had planned for me. Secondly, I had on a tattered old sweater and looked rather raggedy for my father's return. I didn't care—my father was home.

The world began its gigantic transformation from total war in 1945. In January, commercial air service across the Atlantic was resumed and in August, private wartime flying restrictions along the eastern seaboard were rescinded. On August 17 the War Department sent out 4,500 telegrams to aircraft manufacturers in eleven northeastern states canceling aircraft contracts. At the end of 1945, the Army and Navy had canceled a total of $26.6 billion worth of aircraft purchase commitments.

Consolidated Vultee Aircraft Corp. in its Wayne, Michigan plant reverted to the civilian market and started production of its four-place Stinson Voyager. Douglas Aircraft Company produced the DC-4 and DC-6 commercial airliners. The DC-4 was the civilian version of the Army's C-54 Skymaster. Lockheed Aircraft Corp., after termination of its military contracts, continued experimental contracts for the Army on the P-80 Shooting Star jet fighter. Meanwhile its production lines were turning out the Model 649 Constellation airliner, affectionately known as the Connie.

While on leave at the end of February 1946, my father was able to log hours flying out of Long Beach Army Airfield (AAF). He flew a Consolidated B-24M heavy bomber and a

North American B-25J medium bomber. He also spent time in the familiar C-47 transport. Why would he spend his leave flying? I'm sure he knew it was to be his last time as pilot of military aircraft. On March 21 he was honorably discharged from the USAAF at the separation center, Fort MacArthur, California.

Kenneth, all dressed up with no place to go; 1348th ATC – Myitkyina, Burma (1945)

Kenneth with souvenir Japanese sniper rifle

1352nd AAF Base Unit, ATC Search and Rescue, Mohanbari, India
(1945)

Kenneth in front of
his tent in Tent Row,
Mohanbari, India
(1945)

Search and Rescue C-47

Kenneth standing next to a Search and Rescue UC-64 Norseman

North American B-25J Bernice. Kenneth flew this type of aircraft most of the time while in Search and Rescue.

Kenneth at the controls of a North American B-25J (note Search and Rescue insignia)

Kenneth's "Short Snorter." Beginning early in WWII, airmen in America's Army Air Forces autographed each other's dollar bills, usually a Silver Certificate, after leaving on their first trip overseas. As they traveled the world, paper money from each new country was added and more autographs collected. Not only were the bills signed over the oceans, but also while flying the Hump. Signing was clumsy because of the oxygen masks required at high altitudes. The owner was obligated to show the "Short Snorter" on demand. If he didn't, the penalty was usually picking up the tab for a round of drinks.

Chapter 9
Sea of Change

Mechanic, Pilot, Service Chief
He strove to find his place
As the world emerged from war
Re-forming at a hectic pace

On March 5, 1946, just a few days prior to my father's discharge from the Army Air Force, world history took another dynamic turn. Former British Prime Minister Winston Churchill declared, " . . . an iron curtain has descended across the [European] continent." He said this in a speech given in Fulton, Missouri, in response to the Union of Soviet Socialists Republic (USSR) dictator Joseph Stalin's actions and statement that a war between Capitalism and Communism was inevitable. America's wartime ally had become its next adversary.

In April, my father opened his own aircraft repair shop at Indio Airport in Indio, California. He called his new business "Chastain's Aircraft Service." He maintained and repaired private aircraft, as well as aircraft owned by the airport management. He also obtained licenses for several war surplus aircraft, flying them to Tri-City Airport in San Bernardino, where he filled out the proper paperwork and had the planes inspected.

He test-hopped all repaired aircraft and flew charter flights for the airport's management. There were times when my father let me jump into the open front cockpit of a Stearman PT-17 and go up with him on a check ride.

The planes my father flew out of Indio were many: Aeronca 7AC Champions, the Aeronca TA and 11AC Chief, the Taylorcraft BL and B-12, the Stinson 10-A and 108 Voyager, the Ryan PT-22, the Fairchild PT-19, the Stearman PT-17, and the Vultee BT-13.

It was during this time that my parents sold our house in Lakewood Village and I was very upset about it. When we first moved to Indio in March, we lived in a small camper trailer in front of the airport hangar. A shower was built inside the hangar for us to use, but living was cramped and uncomfortable. I missed our Lakewood Village home very much.

It wasn't long though before we moved into a rented house in nearby Cathedral City. I remember the street in front of the house was dirt and there was cactus everywhere. I carry a vivid picture in my mind of lying across my mother's lap while she pulled cactus needles out of my rear end. I was also told to shake my shoes out every morning before I put them on to ensure a scorpion hadn't crawled into them during the night. I hated desert living with a passion.

One day, flying in a war surplus Ryan PT-22, a family landed at Indio Airport and had my father check the plane for some reason. In the course of his inspection he noted the Ryan had a cracked wing spar (main wing support). He recommended it be repaired right away. Despite my father's warning, the owner of the plane decided to wait until he got to his destination before having it repaired. Unfortunately, he didn't make it. We read in the paper the next day he had crashed in the hills, killing himself and taking his wife and young daughter with him.

There were several crop dusters flying out of that airport. One evening a Piper Cub Super Cruiser that had been modified for crop-dusting was hauled in for my father's inspection. As happened with many crop duster aircraft, this one had hit a telephone wire or a tree and crashed. Although the plane was literally in pieces, my father utilized his vast skills and experience to help put it back together. It was soon dusting crops again.

With the end of the war, domestic air travel was once again taking off. By that time, domestic airlines had made purchase commitments for 554 new transports. Seventy-one million dollars worth of Army surplus airplanes had been converted into commercial transports. As a sign of the coming jet age, the pilot ejector seat, designed to catapult a pilot from the cockpit of high-speed airplanes, was tested by the Army at Wright Field. Additionally, the first commercial helicopter license was issued by the CAA to Bell Aircraft Company in 1946.

Due to poor airport management, my father was forced to close his aircraft repair shop in August. To clear his mind after having to give up his business, he took a few flights in a friend's Ercoupe out of Ontario, California. Fortunately, though, he soon received an offer from a Stinson and Aeronca aircraft distributor called "Western States Aviation."

We moved to 112 S. Rose in Burbank, California and my father became Service and Parts Manager, responsible for all functions of the service shop and spare parts departments of Western States Aviation. Fortunately, he still was able to fly as a part of his job. He flew customers' planes to analyze any difficulties and he test flew all newly assembled or repaired aircraft. He spent many hours in Aeronca 7AC Champions. He also flew Aeronca 11AC Chiefs, Stinson 108 Voyagers, and the Stinson's wood-paneled version called the Flying Station Wagon.

There was an instance when my father had repaired a North American AT-6A and was taking it up for a checkout ride over Glendale Airport. Just after he was airborne, he pulled back the prop pitch lever all the way. ("Pitch" is the angle of the propeller as it cuts through the air.) He had done this many

times in the numerous BT-13s he had flown in the past; however, unlike the BT-13, in an AT-6A, pulling the pitch lever
all the way back put the propeller in high pitch mode. This
made the engine shake violently. My father quickly moved the
lever back to the forward position, stopping the vibration. He
continued on his way, having learned another valuable lesson
in the complex world of aviation.

The Stinsons that were sold by Western States Aviation were
manufactured in Wayne, Michigan and flown fully assembled
to Glendale, California. On the other hand, the Aeroncas were
manufactured in Middletown, Ohio and transported partially
assembled by railroad boxcars to Glendale, where they were
offloaded. After their final assembly was completed at Western
States Aviation, it was my father's job to take them up for a
test ride.

Nineteen forty-six saw another glimpse of things to come
in the form of the ENIAC computer. The ENIAC ("Electronic
Numerical Integrator and Calculator") weighed thirty tons and
took up a whole room. Built at the University of Pennsylva-
nia, the War Department of the United States planned on using this 18,000 vacuum tube monster for, among other things,
artillery calculations. Meanwhile, International Business Machines (IBM) developed plans for designing a less powerful
calculator for commercial use.

Across the country, new homes were being built to help
satisfy the returning servicemen's post-war demand for housing. My parents were a part of this surge for housing and purchased a new home in San Fernando (now Sylmar). They
moved to 5737 Elmer in North Hollywood, California in January of 1947 and lived there until their new home was completed. In the meantime, I stayed with some people near the
school I would be attending after the move to San Fernando.
I lived with these strangers until my family was reunited in
March at 13150 Aztec Street.

The war's end was being felt more and more by the average American citizen as wartime wage and price controls were lifted, with the exception of rent and sugar. Of the 500 or more training fields the Army Air Forces had during the war, only three were still in active operation. The National Security Act of 1947 became law on July 26, establishing the Department of Defense with its three military departments—Army, Navy, and Air Force.

On September 18, 1947, W. Stuart Symington was sworn in as the first Secretary of the United States Air Force, establishing it as a separate military branch from the Army. The USAAF my father knew was history.

In September, Stinson Aircraft Corporation was purchased by Convair, which withdrew all distributorships and appointed direct factory dealers. My father went to work for Stinson as Regional Service Manager. He periodically flew a company-furnished demonstrator to all the dealers in the Western Region. He demonstrated the aircraft to prospective customers and made regular reports to the main office in Wayne, Michigan.

Also in September, my father flew a brand new 1948 model Stinson with a 165-HP Franklin engine from the factory in Wayne, Michigan to Glendale, California via Cincinnati, Kansas City, and Tucumcari, New Mexico. While flying near Mormon Lake, south of Flagstaff, Arizona, his plane started losing altitude. He thought it was because of a strong down draft. Shortly thereafter he entered an area of updraft, so he stayed in that general area, circling while he regained altitude.

Upon his arrival in Glendale, he found out he wasn't the only pilot of a new Stinson who had experienced sudden loss of altitude. It turned out the gas cap on top of the wing had a rear-facing vent that allowed too much air to evacuate the gas tank, affecting engine's performance. When the plane began losing altitude, the natural reaction is to pull back on the wheel, increasing the angle of attack. This, in turn, increases the vacuum above the wing, exacerbating the problem. After changing gas cap types, he had no further problems of this sort.

Nineteen forty-seven was also the year pilot Chuck Yeager broke the sound barrier in a Bell X-1 rocket plane. Expressly built to furnish data on the type of problems encountered by an aircraft at or above the speed of sound, the X-1 was purely a research plane. It was powered by a Reaction Motors rocket engine, had very thin, straight wings and tail-plane, and a fuselage shaped like a .50-caliber bullet.

As a sign the Jet Age had arrived in military aviation, three significant new jet-powered bombers, originally tested for the Army Air Forces, were revealed in the latter part of that year. They were the Boeing XB-47 six-jet bomber called the Stratojet, the Northrop YB-49 eight-jet bomber called the Flying Wing, and the soon-to-be-famous Boeing XB-52 Stratofortress heavy bomber.

America's first contribution to the field of operational jet fighters, the Lockheed P-80 Shooting Star, was now fully operational, replacing the P-47 Thunderbolt. The North American XF-86 Saber jet fighter made its first flight on October 1, 1947. The "P" designation for "Pursuit" had changed to "F" for "Fighter." The Saber was America's first swept-wing fighter and became the first U.S. fighter to exceed a speed of Mach1.

Also in 1947, United Helicopters unveiled its "Hiller 360" in Palo Alto, California. A three-place helicopter, it had been designed by Stanley Hiller, who eventually formed his own company, Hiller Helicopters. My father would work there.

My father continued working for Stinson Aircraft until mid-January 1948, at which time he took a position as Service Manager for Brown Automobile Company in Van Nuys, California. This was a DeSoto and Plymouth dealership. Because of my father's "Hump pilot" experience, Howard Brown had made him an offer my father believed was better than the job he had with Stinson, so he took it.

On January 4, 1948, after 62 years of British rule, Burma became an independent state. It was the country my father had flown from during the war. Just a few months later, on May 14, the State of Israel, a former British protectorate, was established. The very next day war between the Arabs and the Jews began, starting a conflict that still exists today.

On April 3, 1948, President Truman signed the Marshall Plan. This innovative action allocated billions of dollars to rebuild war-ravaged Europe. The plan, urged by Secretary of State George Marshall, was an effective way of averting massive starvation and economic depression in Europe. It was also the basis for the global strategy of limiting the expansion of Communism. America's prewar feelings of isolationism, an attitude held since the nation's birth, were laid to rest as America took on the role of world leader.

The first major test of America's new leadership role began on June 26 of that year. The Soviets began a blockade of Berlin, which was surrounded by Soviet-controlled-and-occupied Germany. In response, the United States Air Force dispatched squadrons of transport planes to Germany to carry food and supplies into that beleaguered city. The Air Force's vast experience transporting supplies to China over the Hump was utilized in organizing what was to be called the "Berlin Airlift."

Because he had been one of those brave pilots who flew the Hump during the war, my father was a part of that early air transport learning process. Of course, being involved took him away from his family, as did most of his flying activity. Because of his frequent absences, I have only fleeting memories of him when I was very young, but despite the fact that his flying and wartime responsibilities kept him away from home, there must have been some level of connection between him and me. Of course, I would have liked more.

I have always been aware of my father's love for music. He especially liked the big bands. He played the trumpet and had a large collection of 78-rpm records. He didn't mind me playing them when I was a boy. Being an only child, I was alone much of the time, so playing records was a way to escape boredom. I didn't read a lot in my younger years. I don't remember a lot of books around the house, but the music was there and I sampled it all.

I remember listening to Glenn Miller, The Ink Spots, Benny Goodman, The Mills Brothers, Phil Harris, and The Three Suns. I even remember Frankie Carl's cocktail piano. I've kept the interest in music I developed while listening to my father's records with me all my life. As new styles of music were introduced to me, I branched out, but I have never lost my love for the music my father had in his record collection. Perhaps it provides me with some level of connection to him.

Kenneth beside a North American AT-6. He also flew and repaired this type of aircraft in Indio (1996).

Maintenance
Repair

CHASTAIN'S AIRCRAFT SERVICE
Indio Airport
INDIO, CALIFORNIA

Owned and Operated by
K. L. CHASTAIN   PHONE 7519

Kenneth in front of a Ryan PT-22. He repaired and flew planes like these in Indio (1996).

Chapter 10
Tragedy

She was my rock, my stability
My guiding light both night and day
Then without warning she was gone
When the Angels came and took her away

Although I wasn't as close to my father as I would have liked, I do have vivid memories of my mother. My mother was always there for me—always a part of my consciousness. When my father went to Burma, my mother and I spent our time together and when my father came back, I remained closer to her than to my father. She did things with me like participate in Cub Scout activities or take me to see the Cisco Kid and Poncho at a local park, whereas my father went to work and did things with my mother, but I don't recall him doing much with me. I'm sure it wasn't purposeful. I do remember he had a special whistle to call me when I was to come home, but for some reason, my father and I weren't as connected as my mother and I were.

I remember when I was around eight years old I was playing in the dirt with a toy truck or something while my mother planted flowers next to me. I remember talking to my mother about sending away for a secret ring offered by some cereal company. I also remember taking trumpet lessons, getting frustrated while practicing and jamming my father's trumpet down, bending it. My mother took it in for repair and never told my father what I had done. We were very close.

We had a washing machine with a motorized ringer on it in our garage. I remember my mother telling me not to stick my hand in the ringer while she went back in the house for some reason. After she was inside, I went to the back door, kneeled down and said in a falsely panicked voice, "Help, I caught my hand in the ringer!" She came running out, petrified. I immediately confessed I was only kidding, but I felt awful that I had frightened her so much.

Because we were so close, when I saw her being wheeled out of my grandmother's apartment on a gurney, I was startled. I went up to her and asked, "What's the matter?" My mother told me she had to go to the hospital for a while, but she would be back soon. In fact, she didn't come back at all.

On September 11, 1948, at the age of 29, my mother died in the hospital of uremia due to malignant nephrosclerosis (kidney malfunction). Because children weren't allowed to visit in hospitals at the time, I never was able to see my mother again. I hated hospitals for their cruelty; I had lost my mother and couldn't even say goodbye to her. My mother's sister, Nita, told me that in her delirium, my mother said she had seen the angels and they were coming back for her. They did.

I've been told that immediately after my mother died my father went to the airport, got in a plane and took off. The family wasn't sure what he had in mind. They were concerned about what he planned to do in his grief. I was completely unaware of what was going on. Being the aviator he was, my father went to the place he knew he could be alone with his thoughts. Up there among the clouds he grappled with the reality of my mother's death—alone. He wasn't in a position to help me deal with this tragedy; I had to do it myself. Being an only child with a pilot father who was gone a lot, I was used to being alone much of the time, but until then, I'd had my mother to provide me love and support. I found myself suddenly and completely alone.

Immediately after the funeral I stayed on an avocado ranch in Southern California with the parents of one of my father's friends. They were complete strangers to me, but they treated me fine. After two or three months there, I moved in with my father's parents, Ann and Everett. Their house was located at 1258 Kassebaum Avenue in El Monte, California.

After my mother's death, my father decided to begin flying again. In November, he began Link training and air work at Riley Flying Service, Inc. of Monrovia, California. He did this in order to attain an Instrument rating. The air work was done in the LAX (Los Angeles), LBB (Long Beach), RIV (Riverside), and PMD (Palmdale) Ranges, flying 1948 Stinsons. He passed his instrument flight test on November 29.

Chuck Nickell of Glendale, California was my father's friend from his early flying days and one of the pilots with whom he'd flown the Hump. Chuck's brother-in-law, Harry Conover, also served in CBI and was the Chief Pilot out of Chanyi, China. After the war, Harry became Chief Pilot of a scheduled California intrastate airline called Airline Transport Carriers. Through this connection, my father was able to get a job there as a copilot.

One of the businesses Airline Transport Carriers ran was called California Central Airlines. My father first flew for Cal Central, which ran service primarily between Burbank and San Francisco, but for a short period of time, also served Sacramento, Oakland, and San Diego. Flying DC-3s, my father flew as copilot. He also alternated in the left, or pilot's seat, with all of the captains.

Airline Transport Carriers also owned a non-scheduled airline. From December 14, 1948, to May 1949, my father was copilot on DC-3s flying between Kansas City and New York. Cities where he landed included, among others, Chicago, Pittsburgh, Cleveland, Detroit, Newark, and St. Louis. During that time my father was technically living with my grandparents and me on Kassebaum Avenue in El Monte, but because he was flying in the East, most of the time he stayed in hotels. Once again, his flying duties kept me from spending any time with him.

Little did anyone notice at the time, but Bell Laboratories announced the invention of the miniature transistor in 1948. By replacing the vacuum tube, this device revolutionized electronic equipment and eventually fostered an industry that not only became a driving force in the world economy, but also provided me with a career when I reached adulthood.

At the end of World War II, the Chinese Nationalists and Chinese Communists resumed their hostilities. Although outnumbered four to one, the Chinese Communists prevailed, due to the corruption and incompetence of the Nationalists. On October 1, 1949, the victorious Chinese Communist leader, Mao Zedong, declared the establishment of the People's Republic of China.

On September 23 of that same year, President Truman announced the Soviet Union had also made and exploded an atomic bomb. The monopoly the United States had enjoyed in the new Atomic Age was over and the U.S. – USSR arms race became deadlier than ever. The founding of the North Atlantic Treaty Organization (NATO) in 1949 served as a means of mutual defense for the Western world, allied against the post-war aggressiveness of the Soviet Union.

Nineteen forty-nine also saw the successful completion of the first non-stop, around-the-world flight in a U.S. Air Force B-50 bomber named *Lucky Lady II*. Refueling four times in the air, it took the plane and its crew of fourteen 94 hours to complete the circuit. The B-50 Superfortress was a variant of the famous Boeing B-29 Superfortress of World War II fame. Among the differences between the B-50 and its namesake were more powerful engines, redesigned engine nacelles, a taller fin and rudder, and a new undercarriage for higher operating weights.

Also in 1949, Northwest Airlines became the first U.S. scheduled airline to serve alcoholic beverages in flight within the United States. Pan American Airways took delivery of the first Boeing 377 Stratocruiser for use as a transoceanic air liner. It had two decks, the lower deck containing a luxurious lounge and bar.

The Stratocruiser was a further leveraging of the B-29/B-50 design. The engines and whole wing and tail structures were the same as the B-50. However, the fuselage was a double-bubble section. The U.S. Air Force called it the C-97 Stratofreighter and utilized it as a troop carrier. Modified further, it was used as a tanker aircraft for air-to-air refueling.

Douglas Aircraft made considerable advancements in the field of transport aircraft with the development of the DC-6A Liftmaster. This evolutionary version of the DC-4 was also used by the United States Air Force. Designated the C-118, Liftmasters began providing comfortable air travel to enlisted men and their dependents for the first time in history. One of these planes was used by President Truman and named *Independence* after his hometown of Independence, Missouri.

In May of 1949, my father began flying directly for California Central Airlines. He flew out of Burbank, California. Cities on his route were San Diego, San Francisco, Oakland, and Sacramento. Interspersed with these flights he made several trips from Burbank to New York and back, flying for Airline Transport Carriers.

A June 1 survey showed that in the month of May, for the first time in history, more people in the United States traveled by air than by first-class train. My father was a participant in this giant leap in transportation. During slack periods, he flew

DC-4s as a copilot for Great Lakes Airlines, C-46s for Trans-America Airlines and, as Captain, DC-3s for North American Airlines. He also performed part-time duties as an aircraft dispatcher for Cal Central, obtaining dispatcher's license #1176802. For pleasure, he flew an Aeronca Champion and made many flights out of Vail Field in a Twin Cessna. From time to time he also flew a Lockheed Lodestar out of Burbank Airport.

On April 27, 1950, Transcontinental and Western Air, Inc. changed its corporate name to Trans World Airlines, Inc. My father worked for TWA in his first job after leaving the Army back in 1936. In 1939 Trans World Airlines' design requirements led to the development of Lockheed's Constellation airliner. In 1950, Lockheed Aircraft Corp. began producing an enlarged and improved version of the famous Connie called the Super Constellation. The Super-Connie was 18 feet longer than its predecessor and could carry 76 first-class passengers.

On June 25, 1950, North Korean soldiers in Soviet tanks charged across the 38th parallel on the divided Korean peninsula. This line separated the communist North from the non-communist South. In response, under a United Nations mandate to protect South Korea, President Truman sent in U.S. troops. Commanded by General Douglas MacArthur, the American forces began pushing the North Koreans back to the north. However, Communist China, feeling more threatened by the American Army's presence than was understood at the time, joined the North Koreans. In a massive invasion, the Chinese troops killed thousands of U.S. troops and forced them into a major retreat to the south. The so-called "police action" had turned into the Korean War.

I was still living with my grandparents at that time and not really aware of what was going on in Korea. During the summer I was sent from Southern California to Sacramento to spend part of the summer with my father's younger sister, Neita, and her family. While I was there, my father married Evelyn Arthur of San Leandro, California. Neita, who had been living in that area, had introduced my father to Evelyn. He and Evelyn were married on July 29, 1950.

Kenneth and Ken Jr. at 13150 Aztec San Fernando (now Sylmar) (1948)

Mercedes and Ken Jr. just prior to her death (1948)

Mercedes Chastain (1918–1948)

Chapter 11
Stepmother

He was a man alone
Having lost his wife
So he chose another mate
To help him get through life

I was eleven when my father remarried. It came as a complete surprise to me. I had never heard of this lady when my father announced he'd married her. In the time between my mother's death and my father's new marriage, I had been bounced around somewhat. I didn't have the benefit of my father's influence because he was always gone flying. I had been mostly doing my own thing—alone, as usual.

Before I knew it I was living in Northern California where I had never been before, staying in a strange woman's apartment at 370 Estudillo Avenue in San Leandro. Suddenly I had to adjust to a completely new way of life, without any forewarning and without any support from the main person in my life—my father.

I hated my stepmother at first. While I had previously lived life rather loosely, she was very strict. While I had been without structure in my life, she demanded unbending compliance.

While I had lived mostly within myself, she spent hours talking to me. This new reality was strange and very uncomfortable.

Because my father was unable to take charge of my life, my stepmother stepped in by default. She required I become responsible. She made me aware of the consequences of my actions. All of this was very difficult to deal with. My internal struggle with the many changes in my life made me wish my father had never married this woman.

It took me about two years to begin to see the light. Over time, the newfound stability in my life began to pay dividends. Looking back on this period, I feel a deep gratitude for the dose of reality my stepmother gave me at a critical juncture in my life. I am grateful I was spared a life of drifting, a life of little promise because of my lack of direction. It's funny how life works sometimes. This sudden change, this overwhelming shock, became a defining moment in my young life.

As it turned out, Evelyn and my father had flying in common, though to a lesser extent on my stepmother's part. When she was in her mid-twenties, she had gone to work in the shipyards. The world was at war, and like millions of other women, Evelyn wanted to do her part. She worked as secretary for the Materials Manager at one of the shipyards building "liberty ships" in Richmond, California.

It was there she met a friend, Alice Reed. They partied together and there were lots of parties. On the job it seemed as if everyone was given "make work" tasks and Alice and Evelyn got bored. During this period, women fliers were being publicized in *Life* magazine and other media. Women Airforce Service Pilots (WASP) were ferrying AAF planes from factories to stateside air bases, freeing male pilots for the battlefronts. It's not surprising that in this atmosphere Evelyn and Alice decided they'd like to learn to fly.

They'd heard of a flying school in Alturas. Because civilian flying was banned along the coast during the war, flight schools were located further inland. Alturas sits in the north-east corner of California, in the mountains and far from the coast. Evelyn and Alice wrote to the flying school and on November 17, 1943 the owner, M.N. Gustavson, wrote the following in reply:

DEAR MISS REED AND MISS ARTHUR:

THANK YOU FOR YOUR LETTER OF NOVEMBER 15. WE WILL BE ON HAND TO MEET YOU AT THE SOUTHERN PACIFIC STATION AT 7:55 A.M. MONDAY, NOVEMBER 22, AND WILL MAKE HOTEL RESERVATIONS FOR THAT EVENING.

WE ARE HAPPY TO KNOW THAT YOU FIND IT POSSIBLE TO COMMENCE FLYING AT THIS TIME AND WILL DISCUSS THE MATTER UPON YOUR ARRIVAL.

YOURS VERY TRULY,
M.N. GUSTAVSON
GUSTAVSON FLYING SERVICE

On the strength of the letter they gathered up their courage, hopped the train in nearby Emeryville, and rode it up over the Sierra Nevada Mountains, down through historic Donner Pass and into Reno, Nevada. The next day two pilots from Gustavson Flying Service picked them up to fly them to Alturas. Since there were two of them plus the pilots, the flying school had sent two Piper Cubs. The little Piper Cubs only had room for two—the pilot and one passenger.

Because this was an important occasion for the two women, they dressed up. Evelyn wore high heels, a skirt, and blouse. For protection against the November weather, she also wore a fur coat made from gray squirrel. Alice climbed into one plane with her pilot and Evelyn climbed into the other plane with her pilot, Marty. They took off from Reno, heading north. Everything went okay until they neared their destination when, all of a sudden, Evelyn's plane was enveloped in a dense overcast.

Marty looked for a hole in the clouds. He wanted to get under the overcast to gain his bearings. Unsuccessful, he kept flying north, straining his eyes to find a way out of their predicament. Finally, he was able to let down and land—in a cow pasture. Evelyn and Marty got out of the plane and hiked through the field to find help. Evelyn struggled to keep up in her skirt and high heels. They climbed a fence and continued tromping through the clinging dirt. Finally, they came to a farmer's house. The farmer was kind enough to drive them to the nearest town, Fort Bidwell.

They had landed in the Fort Bidwell Indian Reservation, located ten miles from the Nevada border and ten miles from the Oregon border. The local populace thought these two, who had dropped in from the sky, were angels from heaven. After Marty called the flight school to tell them they were fogged in, they were asked to go to the local school and give a talk to the kids about flying. Evelyn just listened. Afterward, because of insurance reasons, Evelyn was driven to the flight school. Marty flew the plane back after the weather cleared. Alice had been the fortunate one—her pilot had found a hole in the clouds and landed at their intended destination.

Gustavson's Flying Service was a private, pay-as-you-go school. Ten to twelve students attended while Evelyn was there, most of them women. The men were overseas fighting the enemy. Evelyn and Alice rented a furnished house for a while. Other than furniture, there wasn't much in the house. Because they didn't have a coffeepot, they used the water they boiled eggs in to make coffee.

They were each assigned an instructor and time to fly. Having no transportation, they walked from the house to the flying field. Evelyn's first time up was on November 26, 1943, in a Taylorcraft, Certificate Number 27605. A familiarization flight, it lasted twenty minutes. She continued flying with an instructor on a daily basis from the next day on.

Being late fall in the very northern part of California, the plane cabins were very cold. There were heaters in them but they didn't work. These were not exactly the newest of planes. To protect herself against the cold, Evelyn wore long johns under her clothing.

When the first snow of the year came, Evelyn happened to have left some long johns hanging out on the clothesline. The next morning they were frozen stiff. One weekend she and Alice ran out of heating oil. Oil was delivered only during the week, so for more than two days they nearly froze to death. When they did get heating oil, they threw a party to celebrate.

During that time Alice was married, but she left the flight school sometime later and went to Reno to get a divorce. However, she did eventually return and finish the course. Even though Evelyn had lost her roommate and was running low on money, she stuck with her flying lessons. During Christmas break she went home to Oakland for the holidays and borrowed some money. On returning to Alturas she moved in with the town sheriff and his wife, so she wasn't alone. As in Richmond, parties abounded.

Gustavson's Flying Service had a total of three or four planes—Taylorcraft and Piper Cubs. Besides the owner, Gustavson, there were three instructors. Evelyn's first instructor was a woman who was very good at what she did. Students had to be at the field one hour before flight time.

Although Evelyn was myopic, she flew without her glasses. As a result, whenever she landed, she continually flared out ten feet above the runway. After going around the flight pattern a number of times, always flaring out ten feet high her instructor asked, "Do you have a problem seeing?" Evelyn glanced back at her instructor and confessed, "I wear glasses," to which the instructor replied, "Then wear them." After that she landed properly.

Another time Evelyn came in for a landing, making a perfectly smooth three-point touchdown. After the landing she taxied to the hanger area. On the way a wheel strut broke. The wing dropped to the ground, crumpled and the wooden propeller splintered. Because the landing was fine, it wasn't Evelyn's fault. Her instructor said to her, "These things happen all the time."

One day, coming in after practicing maneuvers for a couple of hours with her instructor, it started to snow. There was a plane in the landing pattern ahead of them occupied by a woman flying solo. Even though the woman had her license, she hadn't been shown how to land in snow. Seeing the woman's predicament Evelyn's instructor took control of their plane and landed ahead of the other pilot. She first touched the tail down to gain stability then let the front wheels settle onto the snowy runway. Seeing this, the other pilot was able to land.

Evelyn had noticed that when one of her instructors came in too high while landing, he side-slipped the plane to lose excess altitude. When she took her solo flight, she went around the flight pattern as instructed. As she was about to land, she realized that once again, she was too high. She asked herself, *What did the instructor do when he was too high? Oh yes, he side-slipped,* so Evelyn side-slipped the plane.

After she landed, her male instructor went crazy. "What were you doing?" he asked. "A low wing like that can get you in a lot of trouble."

Evelyn responded, "That's what you did when you came in too high."

All during that time Evelyn worked in order to pay for her lessons and living expenses. She worked at a bowling alley sandwich shop that provided some of her meals and allowed her to bowl a lot. She worked at a department store. She worked at a creamery where she gained twenty pounds finishing off milkshakes and also served meals in a restaurant.

One evening Evelyn went to the movies and saw a war picture in which P-40 fighters were "peeling off." Feeling more confident in her flying by then, she decided she would try peeling off in a Taylorcraft. She had no idea how to do it, but she was determined to try. Flying at the 3,000-foot minimum altitude, Evelyn put her little plane into a stall. She then kicked the rudder to one side so the wing would drop off. The plane peeled off nicely. Her instructor saw this maneuver, of course. After she landed he demanded to know, "What were you doing?" When she explained, he said, "Do you know a Taylorcraft's wings aren't stressed for that?"

While practicing flying one day, Evelyn was making her landing approach on the down-wind leg of the pattern. She was feeling overly confident (because by that time she thought she was a hotshot pilot). As she looked out the left window, she throttled back with her right hand to start her descent. Because she did this without looking, she inadvertently pulled the lever that shuts off the gas to the engine, rather than the throttle. As she watched, the plane's propeller slowed and then stopped. Surprised, she looked up to see telephone wires stretched across her path at the beginning of the runway. Why were they always placed there?

She had to decide in an instant whether to go over or under the wires. She believed she had enough altitude to make it. *Besides, she thought, if I dive under the wires, I'll most likely pick up too much speed and overshoot the runway.* She went over the wires without a problem—"dead stick" (without power). Because she didn't have any power, she didn't come in too high and made a perfectly smooth landing. Those little Taylorcraft could float a long way without power.

As this was happening, the mechanics outside the hangar smoking cigarettes saw the dead stick landing unfold. They went running up toward the plane most likely thinking it was going to hit the wires. When Evelyn landed safely, they seemed very happy the plane wasn't broken. After all, they would be the ones who would have to put it back together again.

There was a woman pilot who had a habit of cutting people off. One day Evelyn was just about to enter the landing pattern when she saw another plane ahead of her. She circled out of the pattern to give the other pilot a chance to land. As the second plane entered the pattern, the woman pilot cut right in front of it and landed. She did this one time too many, however. FAA reps periodically visited the field to inspect the flight school. Once when they were there, the woman cut someone else off. She was not seen around there again.

Normally it took sixteen hours of flying to qualify for a pilot's license. It took Evelyn eighteen hours because she didn't feel she was ready. For the written part of qualification she had a choice. She opted to take the commercial license test because it was possible to miss more questions and still pass than on the private license test. She had the most trouble learning the Aircraft and Engines (A&E) portion, but managed to pass the complete test with an 80 percent.

For her check ride, Gustavson himself went up with her. One of the maneuvers she had to perform was a two-and-one-half spin. Evelyn did some spins, but wasn't sure how many. Once back on the ground Gus said to her, "Well, ya passed." He wasn't very enthusiastic about it.

After getting her license, Evelyn went to Reno. There she managed to get a job at the Reno Army Air Base as a Link Trainer instructor. A Link Trainer was a World War II method of teaching instrument flying to pilots. One of the men from the flight school flew her down to Reno. At first she stayed with a friend at the Rose Bud where she slept on the sofa.

(The Rose Bud was a rooming house that no longer exists.) After a while she managed to get a neat room she shared with a roommate from England, Loma, who also worked as a Link Trainer instructor.

To become a link instructor, Evelyn had to take a test. She only missed one question in the entire exam. As it turned out, she was correct in her answer to the question that was marked wrong. The question was, "What is the shortest distance between two points?" Her answer was "The arc of the great circle." She was eventually given credit for it.

Evelyn worked as a link instructor for two years. During that time she went up in C-46 and C-47 transports to experience the real thing. She often sat in the right hand seat, the copilot's seat, as the pilot "flew the beam." Both civilians and GIs worked as instructors. All of the students were officers and they often took her to eat at the Officers' Club.

Coming to work one day, she smelled the acrid odor of burning flesh. The smell was everywhere and affected everyone. Two aircraft had collided at the end of the runway and exploded. It was a horrible reminder of what was drummed into every pilot's head . . . Look! Look all around, all the time!

While teaching link, Evelyn decided she'd like to try and get into the WASPs—after all, she now had her pilot's license. She and Loma went to San Francisco to apply. One of the things they had to do was take an eye exam. Of course, Evelyn knew she couldn't pass the eye test. After Loma took her exam, they went to a second doctor and Loma went in and took the exam again, this time saying she was Evelyn Arthur. They sent in their applications and soon got a reply. "Thank you, but there will be no further classes." The war was coming to a close and the WASP program had been cancelled. Pilots returning from overseas were now doing the job.

While in Reno, Evelyn periodically flew Piper Cubs to keep her pilot's license current. After the war she continued flying

Taylorcraft and Piper Cubs out of Concord for a while. Her last flight as a licensed pilot was in a Taylorcraft on December 1, 1946, approximately four years before she met and married my father.

It hadn't been a problem for my father to relocate north because he was flying between Burbank and Oakland, so he could live at either end of the route. Flying that route also allowed him to be a part of a "first" in his sister's life. Late in July on one of his trips from Oakland to Burbank, my Aunt Neita and her children Carole, Johnny and Genie took their first airplane ride in my father's airliner.

My father continued flying for California Central Airlines until August, when he left the carrier to take a better position as Chief Pilot and Captain on a DC-3, flying for C&M Enterprises out of Oakland. For C&M he flew charter and lease flights. He also flew "mystery" flights, where the destination was unknown to the passengers. Unfortunately, the company went bankrupt in November. (I guess people really wanted to know where they were going.) In any event, on October 13, 1950, my father made his last flight in DC-3 License Number 17333. This was to be the last airplane he would fly for over four years.

Evelyn Arthur at Gustavson Flight School (circa 1943)

Evelyn Arthur in a Taylorcraft (circa 1943)

Left to right: Alice and Evelyn, with two other students

Chapter 12
Helicopters, Jets, and *Dilbert*

He sacrificed his craft
To be there for his son
But though his wings were clipped
He still could fly for fun

Over the skies of Korea in November 1950, the United States Air Force emerged victorious in the world's first jet plane dogfight when a Lockheed F-80 shot down a Russian-built MIG-15.

Due in large part to the requirements of the Korean War, in 1950 Hiller Helicopters, Inc. of Palo Alto, California received military orders for modified versions of its civilian Model 360 helicopter. Hiller was formed in 1945 under the corporate name of United Helicopters, Inc. and soon became my father's employer.

First my father took a job as an aircraft mechanic for Transocean Airlines at Oakland Airport. He worked for Transocean for two months while he looked for a better position. He found one in December when he took a job as Commercial Service Manager for Hiller Helicopters. At Hiller he was responsible for the Service Department, which included all functions related to service problems, spare parts, shipping, exporting, and customer complaints. He was also responsible for furnishing technical data, service bulletins and service literature to all commercial customers.

At the end of the year Douglas Aircraft began producing a larger and faster model of the DC-6, the DC-6B commercial airliner, and in 1951, Douglas not only received formal certification for its DC-6B, but also announced the development of an even larger and faster transport designated the DC-7. The DC-7 was the last Douglas airliner powered by piston engines.

Douglas Aircraft also made preparations for tests with the Air Force using its X-3 Stiletto supersonic research plane. This was the first aircraft in the X Series designed to take off and land under its own power. Prior X Series planes were lifted into the air under the belly of a B-29 and then released. The Stiletto was jet powered, had a slender fuselage, a long, tapered nose, and tiny, very thin wings.

My mother's brother and my father's friend, Dewitt Pyeatt, was still working as an engineer at Douglas and was asked to make a few configuration changes to the X-3. He ended up redesigning the entire airplane. His biggest challenge was figuring out where to put the fuel. The X-3's wings were so small and thin they couldn't be utilized for fuel storage. They would only be able to carry about 18 gallons. He managed to place room for 500 pounds of fuel in the fuselage between the two engines. There was only a mock-up and two prototypes made of this aircraft and only one of the prototypes was ever flown.

In 1951, the world's first electronic digital computer was designed for commercial use. Debuting in Philadelphia on June 14, the Universal Automatic Computer (UNIVAC) weighed eight tons and consumed about 100 kilowatts of power. Television's first coaxial cable now stretched across the country and a New York television station broadcast the first baseball game in color.

In December, the atom was put to a peaceful use when a nuclear reactor generated electricity for the first time. On the war front, the Department of Defense reported the losses of 583 U.N. planes to enemy action in Korea as of December 12.

In 1951, for the first time in history, scheduled air passenger miles exceeded the total passenger miles traveled in Pullman railroad cars. The 1950s saw aircraft development and manufacturing grow exponentially. A prime example was Boeing Airplane Company of Seattle, Washington. Celebrating its 35th anniversary, the company unveiled its first prototype model of the B-52 Stratofortress. Additionally, Piper Aircraft Corporation demonstrated its Piper Tri-Pacer.

My father, my new stepmother, and I moved across the San Francisco Bay to 146 E. West 37th Avenue in San Mateo so my father could be closer to his new job at Hiller Helicopters, down the San Francisco peninsula in Palo Alto. According to a company newsletter, Hiller considered my father to have an unusual knowledge of aviation. An article featuring him stated, "This wisdom, along with hard work, was largely responsible for the flow of technical help and parts needed to keep commercial Hillers flying." The newsletter also pointed out, "From Pakistan to Brazil, from Italy to Indo-China, owners of Hillers throughout the world look to Chastain and his staff to expedite parts, answer inquiries on maintenance, and forward new ideas for improving operations."

Hiller Helicopters began producing a two-place helicopter powered by ramjet engines. Called the Hornet, this personal-sized helicopter was designed to sell at $4,900 and could potentially be stored in an average-size garage without folding the main rotor blades.

In 1952, President Truman, tied down with an "unwinnable" war in Korea, announced he would not be a candidate for re-election. This scenario was repeated when President Lyndon Johnson was tied down with the Vietnam War and also chose not to run for re-election.

General Dwight D. Eisenhower became president in 1953. This soldier-turned-statesman was credited with rescuing Europe from Hitler's grip. He defeated his civilian opponent, Adlai Stevenson II, in a landslide victory, winning more votes than any previous candidate. Fondly referred to as "Ike," Eisenhower enjoyed wide appeal. He came across as a friendly, small-town guy who could guide the war-weary nation through the atomic threat of the Cold War. After winning the election, the president-elect made a three-day visit to the United States troops in Korea.

Sony Corporation introduced a pocket-sized transistor radio that year. For the first time, this small, battery-powered device allowed people to carry the experience of radio along with them as they moved about their daily business.

Besides producing the DC-6A cargo plane and the DC-6B airliner, Douglas Aircraft began production of its new DC-7 piston-driven airliner, scheduled for delivery in 1953. Swedish Airways became the first airline from any country to fly a passenger plane over the North Pole and Pan American World Airways announced it had ordered three British Comet jet airliners for delivery in 1956. Meanwhile, Boeing Airplane Company began development of a commercial jet transport with the prototype planned to fly in 1954. The days of propeller-driven airliners were now numbered.

Boeing's XB-52 Stratofortress made its initial flight in April 1952. The innovative strategic bomber was powered by eight turbojet engines and had sweptback wings. The Douglas X-3 Stiletto on which Dewitt Pyeatt did design work completed its first flight at Edwards Air Force Base in California on October 20. Due to inadequate jet engine technology, the sleek-designed aircraft never reached its performance goals.

Missiles were now becoming a major part of military ordnance. The Navy revealed three new guided missile projects scheduled for service use in 1953. These included the Convair Terrier I surface-to-air missile, the Chance Vought Regulus surface-to-surface missile, and the Douglas Sparrow I air-to-air missile. I worked with Terrier Missiles when I joined the Navy in 1958.

Hiller Helicopters, where my father was working, delivered quantities of helicopters to the Armed Services, along with a limited number of UH-12B commercial models.

The country sighed with relief in 1953 when first the Soviet dictator, Joseph Stalin, died, and second, when the Korean War ended. Stalin was responsible for the deaths of millions of people while he was in power and, at the same time, reshaped the face of Eurasia. Little physical or political change resulted from the Korean War. Sadly, there were more than three million casualties during that three-year period.

Also that year the American aviator, Jacqueline Cochran, became the first woman to fly faster than the speed of sound. During World War II Cochran was director of the Women Air Force Service Pilots (WASP). In the 1950s, a woman aviator was referred to as an "aviatrix."

On April 1, 1953, my father, my stepmother and I moved into a brand new home at 551 Cambridge Street in Belmont. The home was located in a housing tract that had recently been the site of an airport. The house cost $10,000. I was very happy about this, having been moved around constantly since my mother died. At long last I was going to have roots. I had a house, a family, a dog, a cat, and the prospect of being able to call Belmont my hometown.

Nineteen fifty-three heralded the fiftieth anniversary of powered flight. Aviation had come a long way from that short hop made by Orville Wright in his Flyer on December 17, 1903. Not only had airplanes become more advanced, they were also much safer. In the late Forties and early Fifties the advent of the jet engine allowed further major advancements in aircraft development. This was because piston-engine aircraft were approaching their performance limits.

On February 1, my birthday, Chance Vought delivered the last propeller-driven military fighter, the Navy F4U Corsair. In March, Boeing's jet transport Project X was ahead of schedule and was expected to be ready for test flight in mid-1954. Boeing also delivered its last propeller-driven bomber, a TB-50H (an advanced version of the famous B-29), to the Air Force and announced from then on, its bomber production would be strictly jets.

On May 7, 1954, French forces were defeated at Dien Bien Phu in French Indochina after a two-month siege by communist Viet Minh troops. At the negotiating table in Geneva, what is now known as Vietnam was divided into two zones. The Communists occupied the zone north of the 17th parallel. The French, who promptly turned over control to the anti-communist forces, occupied the southern zone. Just one month prior to this on April 7, President Eisenhower had announced his "domino theory," which predicted that if one Asian country fell to Communism, the rest were sure to follow. The stage was set for the Vietnam War.

British Overseas Airways Corporation (BOAC), flying the 36-passenger DeHavilland Comet 1, introduced the world's first scheduled jet passenger service on May 2, 1952. Many other airlines wanted to add Comets to their fleets until on May 2, 1953, one crashed on takeoff at Calcutta (Kolkata), India, killing everyone on board. On January 12, 1954, another Comet dived into the sea near Italy, again with no survivors. Then on April 8, 1954, yet another Comet broke up in flight with total fatalities.

All Comets were grounded. From studying pieces of wreckage, it was determined the cause of the crashes was metal fatigue around the square window apertures in the fuselage.

This previously unknown phenomenon resulted in a weakening of the jet's skin causing catastrophic failure. BOAC began to operate with a modified Comet in 1958, but by then it was too late: the Boeing 707 jetliner had made its debut.

The fruits of Boeing's Project X, the Model 707 prototype, made its maiden flight on July 15, 1954. The 146-passenger 707 was America's first jet-propelled transport aircraft. It quickly established itself as one of the great air transports in aviation history. Pan American World Airways was only the first customer of countless others.

When developing the 707, some doubts were raised at Boeing. For instance, could airline pilots, schooled in piston-engine aircraft, make the transition to an airplane whose velocity approached the speed of sound? Later it was found that with adequate training, this was generally not a problem; however, this issue would later affect my father.

Working at Hiller Helicopters offered a special benefit for pilots like my father. The company sponsored a flying club that owned an Aeronca Champion called *Dilbert*. It was named after a newspaper cartoon. He began logging hours in *Dilbert* in 1954, both for pleasure and to keep his flying skills up to par. In 1955, my father and my stepmother flew to Southern California to visit the newly opened Disneyland.

In May of 1955, the Western Allies admitted West Germany into the North Atlantic Treaty Organization (NATO). In response, the Soviet Union and its Eastern European satellites, with the exception of Yugoslavia, formed the Warsaw Pact. West Germany was viewed by the Soviets as an armed threat on the fringes of the Iron Curtain. In the Far East, Ngo Dinh Diem announced he was President of South Vietnam.

Other important events of the year included the first televised presidential press conference. Also, the U.S. Government approved the Salk vaccine, which helped to eradicate a crippling disease—polio. People could now be protected against the disease that caused the paralysis and sometimes death of thousands. Even the late President of the United States, Franklin Delano Roosevelt, had been crippled by polio.

First flown on December 20, 1955, the piston-engine Douglas DC-7C was developed to meet a Pan American World Airways requirement for an aircraft able to fly transatlantic services in both directions. This made the DC-7C the world's first true, long-range, commercial transport; however, its service-life would not be a long one because in October 1955, Pan American ordered twenty of Boeing's 707-120 four-engine jet airliners. American Airlines also ordered twenty of the 707-120s the same month. The production model 707 made its maiden flight December 20, 1957.

In 1955, when I was a teenager, my father handed me one of his manuals on aerodynamics and told me he would give me flying lessons if I studied it. I don't really recall how I responded to this generous offer, but I most likely gave him some sort of lukewarm answer. As I look back, with a lifetime of experiences to help me better understand its significance, I can see my father was taking a very big step. By asking me if I would like him to teach me to fly, he was actually offering me the opportunity to enter his special world.

Before I started any study of aeronautics, my father took me up for a check ride. I remember being at the airport and my father showing me how to do a walk-around on an aging brown and yellow Aeronca Champion. He pointed out all of the things that must be checked before taking off. He emphasized the fact, if something were to go wrong in flight you couldn't get out and fix it. I moved the rudder back and forth with my hands and looked for problems. I moved the elevator up and down. I checked the ailerons. I checked the gas level and I checked the engine for oil leaks. On and on, all around the little Aeronca, I learned what was important to keep a plane airborne. If a plane comes down, it's best if it's by pilot choice.

After completing the walk-around, I climbed into the front seat of the enclosed-cabin, high-winged Aeronca named *Dilbert*. This was the plane owned by the Hiller Helicopters Flying Club my father often flew. "SWITCH OFF." As instructed, I checked that the ignition switch was in the OFF position so my father could prime the engine. He did this by turning the propeller by hand a couple of rotations. "CONTACT." Again, as I was instructed, I turned the ignition switch to ON and repeated, "CONTACT." He placed his hands on the prop and threw his right leg straight out for balance. As he pulled down on the wooden propeller his leg came down as well, allowing more force to be applied to his downswing. The engine quickly engaged.

I could see my father through the transparent disk of the propeller as it cut through the afternoon air. He pulled away the wheel chocks and climbed into the seat behind me. Taking control from his rear position, he taxied the Aeronca to the end of Palo Alto Airport's taxiway. He swung the diminutive craft around and aligned it with the runway. In my forward position I had a clear view of the entire runway stretching out before me. With his foot on the brakes, my father throttled-up the engine. The plane trembled as the rpms increased.

After he was satisfied the engine was running smoothly, my father released the brakes and started the takeoff run. Gathering speed, the airplane first lifted its tail off the runway and then seemed to jump into the air. A disorienting sensation overcame me as I watched the ground slip away below me and the plane's nose became skewed with the runway. As we left the ground, my father told me to look closely for jet aircraft from the Navy fighter base at Moffett Field. I felt my stomach tighten as I craned my neck to look for this unexpected danger.

As we gained altitude, we headed out over the San Francisco Bay, toward the Hayward hills. My father leveled out the plane and pointed its nose toward a mountain peak. He told me to take the stick and keep the plane pointing toward the distant crest while maintaining altitude. I anxiously grabbed the stick and immediately over-controlled. No matter how I moved the controls, I couldn't keep the plane's nose pointed straight. Whenever I managed to correctly point the nose toward the mountain, my father would say, "You're losing altitude." Then, as I tried to settle back into the correct altitude, he would tell me, "Keep the nose straight."

After some time and careful coaxing from my father, I finally realized if I just left the control stick alone, the plane would almost fly itself. Small movements would cause the craft to turn or change altitude. I also learned after moving the stick, it is important to return it to the neutral position. When the wing is dipped to the desired angle for a turn or the nose is pitched up or down to gain or lose altitude, an unwanted roll, dive or stall could result if the stick is not returned to neutral.

While practicing turns, my father instructed me to not keep my head level with the horizon. I had been inadvertently doing this. I guess from his position, I must have looked rather strange with my body upright in the seat and my head at some weird angle. He told me to keep my head aligned with my body, even though the plane was in a bank. With so many things to learn all at once, there was no way I could enjoy myself.

I don't recall much more of that flight. I do remember it was the only lesson he gave me. In order to get more lessons I had to study aerodynamics from his manuals. As a teenager I had cars and girls on my mind, not flying. It must have been very disappointing to my father, though he didn't show it. I never did study aerodynamics.

I have often thought about what I gave up when I let that opportunity pass me by. If I had continued with flying then, perhaps I would have gotten closer to my father. I didn't, however, think about it in those terms at the time. As it turned out, my love was for the water—boats and ships. I never really missed not becoming a *flyer*, but I did miss not taking the opportunity to spend more time with my father.

In 1956, Soviet leader, Nikita Khrushchev, condemned his predecessor, Joseph Stalin, for all of the atrocities Stalin had ordered. Its satellite nations interpreted this move to mean the USSR would be taking a more tolerant stance toward the Warsaw Pact nations' nationalistic desires. Hungary withdrew from the Pact in November. In response, the Soviets sent in 2,500 tanks to quash what was considered to be a rebellion, resulting in thousands of deaths and defections. Not only did this show that the Soviet Union would use force to keep its new empire intact, it also became clear the Western nations would not send military aid.

The first VCR prototype was demonstrated in Chicago, the first transatlantic telephone cable system went into operation, and Dwight D. Eisenhower was re-elected President, all in 1956. Also that year, the first transcontinental helicopter flight was made.

Up to that point, aircraft flying at or above the speed of sound were specially built rocket-powered research planes, but in March 1956, Britain's delta-wing Fairey Delta 2 research aircraft demonstrated that a properly designed airplane powered by an ordinary jet engine could approach and pass the speed of sound with no more noticeable effect than a flicker of needles on the instrument panel. From that moment, it became only a matter of time before airliners were designed to carry passengers at supersonic speeds.

Kenneth at work; Hiller Helicopters (circa 1955)

Chapter 13
Back to the Skies

No longer chained to earth
He flew the skies once more
In his element again
This time in a DC-4

In May 1956, Hiller Helicopters consolidated its Commercial and Military Divisions, eliminating my father's position. Hiller offered Dad an alternate position, but he didn't feel it was acceptable. His only other choice was to leave the company. As a result, from August until September he did contract flying. His flying buddy, Chuck Nickell, provided him a connection with Richfield Oil Company. My father flew DC-3s and Beechcraft 18s around California for Richfield.

Sometimes situations cause time to become an overriding factor in our lives; for instance, when my stepmother's grandmother passed away. I had met her grandmother just once. Her name was Florence Edith Weaver and she was living in Grass Valley, California at the time. Grandma Weaver was the second youngest of thirteen children and had some very interesting stories to tell about living in the Midwest during the building of the Transcontinental Railroad. Her husband had worked as a telegraph operator. They moved west to California in the early 1920s.

Sometime after I met her, Grandma Weaver moved from Grass Valley to Genoa, Texas to be close to her family living there. My stepmother, Evelyn, was concerned that her 86-year-old grandmother had gone home to die. Because of this concern, Evelyn had requested if anything should happen to Grandma Weaver, the family was to wire her immediately. The wire came in September 1956, when I was seventeen. Grandma Weaver had died. Evelyn was very close to her grandmother, even sharing the same December 24 birth date. Despite the fact that we were living far away in Belmont, California, Evelyn was determined to attend the funeral.

My father was between jobs and because both he and Evelyn were licensed pilots, Evelyn suggested the family rent a plane and fly to Genoa, near Houston. Having come from humble roots and out of work, my father didn't want to do that. He thought it too expensive, so Evelyn checked out the airlines to see if it was possible to get to Houston in time for the service. Unfortunately, air travel wasn't as developed nor popular as it is today. There just wasn't enough time to get to Genoa using commercial air travel.

Not the shrinking violet type, Evelyn approached my father again about renting a plane. Time was short and she was going no matter what. He relented and the next day found us at the San Carlos Airport, south of San Francisco. We rented a Piper Tri-Pacer, which accommodated four passengers. As its name implies, the Tri-Pacer had a tricycle landing gear. After filing a flight plan and performing the necessary walk-around, we took off and the race to Genoa was on.

There were four of us in the small cream and green airplane. My father sat in the left front seat, while Evelyn sat in the right. I was in the back seat alongside our little black, mixed-breed dog, Pogo. My father had filed a flight plan for this leg of the trip because we were going to be flying due south over the Tehachapi Mountains of Central California. He normally didn't file a flight plan when flying south over the coast instead of over the mountains, but time was of the essence on this trip.

The ride was extremely choppy over the Tehachapis and I started to get airsick. I felt like a weakling. Bouncing around as we were, Pogo was having no problem. My parents, sitting up front, were also just fine. I alone couldn't handle all the jostling about. I tried to keep my agony to myself for as long as I could, but eventually I admitted I was about to be sick. Evelyn looked around the cabin and found the familiar "urp" cup with which small planes came equipped. She handed it to me and I quickly made good use of it.

After we passed over the mountains, things smoothed out and my stomach quit rebelling as much, but I was still sitting there holding the cup full of what was once my breakfast. Mercifully, we soon started our approach to Palm Springs Airport, but as we descended, the temperature started to rise dramatically. As we made our final approach, I swear the contents of the cup I was holding started to cook.

We landed in Palm Springs to gas up and take advantage of the facilities. As we got out of the airplane we were hit by a blast of heat as if someone had opened a furnace door. The temperature was well over 100 degrees and the black surface of the tarmac was so hot Pogo couldn't walk on it. The heat hurt the pads of her feet. She was scooped up and we all hurried to the General Aviation Terminal.

After refueling, we took off again, headed for Tucson, Arizona. We landed in Tucson without incident and because we were going to stay the night, found a motel room near the airport. Evelyn and I also found a drugstore where we purchased some Dramamine tablets. One bout with airsickness was enough for me.

We got up at four o'clock the next morning, still racing the clock to get to Genoa in time for the funeral service. The sky was pitch black as we were getting the plane prepared for takeoff, but the sun started to rise as we taxied to the end of the runway. As we left the ground I looked out the window and saw some ink-black hills. Like a canvas that had been painted behind them, the sky was a brilliant, deep orange. It was a spectacular Arizona sunrise and an uplifting sight to begin the day.

As we flew east from Tucson, my father radioed to ground control, requesting a flight plan be filed for us from Tucson to Houston. The air controller asked from what airport we had taken off. My father replied, "Tucson." The controller came back with an incredulous, "Impossible. You couldn't have because our radar didn't pick you up and it's very sophisticated. Where are you now?" My father gave the coordinates, but the 1950s "sophisticated" equipment still couldn't pick us up. We were flying low through a pass to avoid having to fly over a mountain range, but the incident didn't instill much confidence in our nation's air control system.

Despite the difficulty in locating us, a flight plan was filed and we continued eastward over Arizona, New Mexico, and Texas. We had to stop in El Paso, Texas for fuel. As we began our approach, my father suddenly made an abrupt turn out of the pattern. Evelyn asked, "Why did you do that?" Shifting his headphones to one side, he replied, "We have an airliner behind us and we're going too slow."

My father always described Texas as "miles and miles of nothin' but nothin'." He was right, but the flat countryside worked in our favor as we raced to Genoa, stopping once more in San Angelo for fuel. The funeral was scheduled for that afternoon and it was going to be close.

Genoa, Texas was a suburb of Houston in the 1950s; now it's a part of that city. Because of its proximity to Genoa, my father closed the fight plan as we flew over Houston. On the other side of the city we started looking for a small airport called Emmett Field. Less an airport and more a "field," friends of Evelyn's late grandmother owned it; but no matter how hard we looked, we couldn't find the place. We passed Ellington Air Force Base and found ourselves out over the Gulf of Mexico.

Feeling the pressure of time, my father turned the plane around and we all started looking for any airport. After wandering all over the area we spotted a small airfield and landed to ask for directions. As we pulled up to the terminal a man came running out, shouting, "Are you the Chastains?"

It seems almost everybody in that area of Houston was looking for us. The man pointed out Emmett Field, "straight ahead, just a few miles away," and we took off. The fact that it was very close to Ellington Air Base had contributed to the difficulty we had spotting it the first time. Fortunately, the service was delayed for us, so we hadn't made the trip in vain, but it had been a close call. After the service I met many people whom I had never seen before and was never to see again. We stayed overnight and left for home the next morning.

Emmett Field was very small. Surrounded by empty fields, it had a single hangar, a barn, two airstrips, and not much else. There was a long airstrip and, crossing that, a short takeoff strip. Looking at the lonely windsock sitting out between the runways, it was clear the correct wind direction for takeoff was down the shorter of the two strips. Evelyn thought we were too heavy to takeoff down the short runway. Not only were there three people and a dog aboard, the plane was full of fuel and at the end of the runway sat a very imposing fence.

At this point my father's male ego kicked in. He said, "We can make it, no problem." After saying our goodbyes to friends and family and doing a walk-around inspection of the plane, we climbed into the Tri-Pacer and started it up. My father taxied the plane all the way back to the barn and turned toward the short runway. He was trying to get as much distance as possible between the fence and us. We needed all the speed that could be mustered. As I sat in the back, completely unaware of the potential danger, my father revved up the engine, at the same time pressing down hard on the brake. As soon as he felt the engine giving all the revolutions it could stand, he released the brake and we went bouncing down the strip.

The fence came up quickly, but just before we reached it, my father suddenly dropped the flaps and the little Tri-Pacer jumped into the air, easily clearing the fence. As is usually the case when pulling that type of maneuver, the plane settled a little once we were over the fence, but fortunately, there was nothing but a field on the other side. He raised the flaps; we gained altitude and circled back over the airport. Then, in a final bit of male bravado, my father buzzed the field. Without filing a flight plan this time, we headed for Phoenix, Arizona, stopping again in San Angelo and El Paso for fuel.

It was dark as we approached Phoenix. As we started our descent for landing my father said, "Turn down the cabin temperature." Evelyn checked and told him, "It's not on." Even after sunset, the temperature in Phoenix was 105 degrees. In 1956, Sky Harbor Airport was very small, not the major terminus it is today. It was so dark that night that my father had to radio the airport tower to have them turn on the runway lights so he could see to land.

After an overnight stay in Phoenix, we made an uneventful flight back to the San Carlos Airport. The whole trip happened so fast it was hard to believe we had done all we had. It was an exciting, but quick adventure. Time had been the overriding factor, but it was an experience that would last a lifetime.

After our return from Texas my father asked George Merrill for a job. George, a pilot my father knew from his non-scheduled airline flying days, happened to work for Resort

Airlines. Resort operated out of Oakland, California. Dad got the job and was a copilot on DC-4s for most of his tenure. Toward the end of his time with Resort, he did move to the left seat as Captain. The airline flew United States Air Force cargo under contract with the government.

Nineteen fifty-seven was a year that could truly be described as the beginning of a new era. It divided the time when airplanes took men and women to the greatest heights imaginable from a time when men could realistically imagine traveling in space. The Soviet Union launched the world's first satellite on October 4, 1957, and the people of the United States fell into a state of shock and apprehension. *Sputnik*, as it was called by the Soviets, was a 184-pound ball. It was equipped with a rudimentary radio transmitter that emitted a faint "beep-beep" as it passed overhead.

Americans gazed up from their yards at the night sky trying to distinguish the satellite from all the stars and listened for the beeps on their radio sets. *Sputnik* gave space exploration the rocket-propelled boost necessary to start the race for space and the Soviets were in the lead. Coincidentally, this happened at the same time the United States and the Soviet Union independently developed an Intercontinental Ballistic Missile (ICBM).

The world of commercial aviation also changed dramatically when the first production Boeing 707-120 jet liners started rolling out of the company's factory. Unfortunately for Ford Motor Company, their claim to fame in 1957 was the Edsel automobile. It would become a prime example of a marketing boondoggle. Dick Clark helped change the American music scene with the television program "American Bandstand." The program lasted so long that Dick Clark, the show's host, became known as the "world's oldest teenager."

My father's world had changed again. He was no longer restrained to the ground. Once more he was in his element, flying for Resort Airlines. Because he was piloting relatively slow piston-engine aircraft, his time away from home was approximately two weeks at a time. After two weeks at home, he was off again on his next two-week trip, flying around the country from Air Force base to Air Force base.

I turned 18 in 1957. I worked part-time on weekends and full-time during the summers at a plant nursery. Because I was employed, I was able to help pitch in with the family's bills during the summer when my father was out of work. As a way of saying thank you, my parents surprised me with a car on my birthday. It was a 1952 brown and cream four-door Chevrolet. Having transportation came in very handy because in June I graduated from high school and in September I started attending Junior College up the San Francisco peninsula in San Mateo. However, my college life was short-lived; I just didn't know what I wanted to do. I didn't have a goal, much less the passion for something, like my father had had at my age, so I joined the Navy.

Kenneth in his Resort Airlines uniform (1956)

Kenneth at the controls of a DC-4 somewhere over Seattle (late 1950s)

Trip to Genoa, Texas. Evelyn kneeling in front with family dog,
"Pogo" and Ken Jr. at far right (1956)

Chapter 14
Christmas Flight

For just a brief moment I joined his world
And witnessed his flying skill
He guided his plane with a steady hand
An impression that's with me still

On March 24, 1958, rock-and-roll singer Elvis Presley was drafted into the United States Army. I remember that date clearly because it's the same day I entered the United States Navy. I thought perhaps the Navy would help me find myself. After joining up, I flew with some other recruits from San Francisco International Airport to San Diego's Lindbergh Field in a Pacific Southwest Airlines (PSA) propeller-driven plane. I remember the seats as large and comfortable and the stewardesses (that's what they were called then) were very friendly. Besides offering us the standard "coffee, tea, or milk," they took time to chat with us.

It was nighttime when the plane approached Los Angeles. The pilot offered anyone who was interested to come up to the flight deck and look around. That's where I was when we crossed over the San Gabriel Mountains. Suddenly, before us lay the Los Angeles basin in all its splendor, lights spreading out in all directions in colorful patterns. It was a new and exciting experience for me. Then we landed in San Diego and a Navy bus picked us up and took us to Boot Camp.

After I graduated from Boot Camp I flew back home for a few days' leave; then it was on to my first assignment, the U.S. Naval Guided Missile Basic Electronics School in Dam Neck, Virginia Beach, Virginia. Once again my parents saw me off at San Francisco International Airport. I flew in a four-engine, piston-powered airplane (most likely a DC-6 or DC-7). First we taxied to the end of the runway. After the pilot was given clearance, we taxied onto the runway into position for our takeoff run. The pilot stopped the plane and with the brakes applied, ran up each of the four engines, one at a time. I remembered my father telling me, "Before takeoff, pilots listen for any engine problems while running them at their maximum rpms."

Once airborne, the stewardesses came around with baskets filled with little boxes, each containing two pieces of Chicklets gum. This standard practice helped passengers deal with changes in cabin pressure. We flew first to Los Angeles before heading east. I remember stopping in Tulsa, Oklahoma and in Chicago. By the time we arrived at Dulles Airport in Washington, D.C. it was midnight. I had a layover of four hours and at that time of night, there was nothing open at the airport. Because the airport was twenty miles from downtown, there was no use taking a taxi into town, so I just tried to stay awake until my 4:00 A.M. plane.

Sometime after four o'clock a Capitol Airlines turboprop plane was pulled up to the terminal, but before we could board, we were told the plane had a problem and we would have to wait for a replacement. By the time we finally got on a working aircraft and flew to Norfolk, Virginia, it was daylight. My cross-country flight had taken me fourteen hours. Coast-to-coast air travel in 1958 was quite an adventure.

In October the National Aeronautics and Space Administration (NASA) was established. Besides its aviation component, NASA brought together research that had previously been handled by the different branches of the military. Its first space project was the investigation of our planet and its atmosphere by means of the *Explorer* series of satellites, which also debuted in 1958.

On October 4, British Overseas Airways Corp. (BOAC), using a Comet 4, launched the first transatlantic passenger jet service from New York to London. The Comet 4 was a modified version of the Comets that had crashed earlier with such international alarm. The cross-ocean trip took less time than it did with a prop plane, but on October 26, BOAC's competitor, Pan American World Airways, sent a Boeing 707 to Paris. Mass air transport had quietly begun its speedy and smooth takeover of the skies from piston aircraft.

It was also in 1958 when an engineer at Texas Instruments invented the computer microchip. Little did people realize at the time the impact this invention would have on the future—it certainly impacted mine.

While on Christmas break from U.S. Naval Guided Missile School in Virginia, I found myself in Alabama. Because I was far away from my West Coast home, a fellow sailor invited me to spend Christmas with him and his family. It was my first Christmas away from home. The South was radically different from what I was used to in California, but the people were very friendly to me and I felt right at home. Surprisingly, there was snow on the ground in Alabama. Where I came from, snow was only found in the mountains. There had also been snow back in Virginia Beach where the Navy school was located. I was amazed the first time I saw snow on the sand dunes.

On the evening of Christmas Day, I decided to call my parents. I soon found myself in a lonely telephone booth, dialing home. My stepmother answered and after exchanging Christmas greetings she told me my father was very close by, in Georgia. In his job as copilot for Resort Airlines, he flew Air Force cargo around to the different air bases under a government contract called "Logair." He'd just happened to fly into Warner Robins Air Material Area in Macon, Georgia and was laying over for the night.

The next thing I knew, I was talking to a long distance operator, asking her help in tracking down my father. I placed a person-to-person call and she was very persistent. First, she located the Air Force Base Duty Officer and asked if he knew where the Logair aircrew was staying. The Duty Officer knew the motel where the crews normally stayed and the operator tried that number. So far I had only spent a dime. Luck was with me and I learned my father was staying there. The motel clerk got him on the phone.

"Hi, Ken." I was excited to hear my father's voice.

"Guess what, Dad? I'm in Alabama." My father seemed happy to hear from me, which made me feel good. It just so happened he was headed west and he surprised me by suggesting I come over to Macon and fly back to California with him for Christmas. Of course, I jumped at the chance. To fly with my father across country in one of his cargo planes was almost too good to be true. The next thing I knew I was on a Trailways Bus headed into the night toward Georgia and a new adventure.

Because my father was copilot on the DC-4 he was flying, he had to ask the pilot's permission for me to go with them. The pilot said it was okay, so I was able to fly alongside them in the jump seat. It also helped I was in my Navy uniform, enabling me to easily get in and out of air bases.

We left Warner Robins the next day. It was dark by the time we flew over Texas, but it was clear and I could see dozens of fires rising into the sky. My father said the fires were oilfield gases being burned off. Sitting there between my father and the pilot, looking out at the Texas night sky highlighted by the burning gases, I imagined flying for a living was a pretty neat thing. When I mentioned this to my father he gave me a very unexpected response. "After doing this for a long time, it's almost like driving a bus," he said. Soon I got some idea of why.

The pilot asked me if I would like to fly the plane. I didn't hesitate. My father got up and I slid into the copilot's seat. I placed my hands on the wheel and indicated I was ready. When the pilot took the plane out of autopilot I immediately felt the heaviness of the controls. Remembering my earlier experience with the little Aeronca, I tried not to over-control. I had some trouble holding the same altitude at first, but finally managed to maintain course and assigned altitude. It was a lot of work. After about fifteen minutes the pilot asked me, "Have you had enough?" Again, without hesitating, I said, "Yes." He put the plane back into autopilot and sat back.

We flew over Texas and into New Mexico, where we landed at an Air Force base in Roswell. While the DC-4 was being either loaded or unloaded, the pilot, my father and I left the base and went to a small hole-in-the-wall Mexican restaurant in town. My father said it was his favorite eating spot whenever he stopped in Roswell. When the waitress came to take our order he said, "I'll have huevos rancheros." I had never heard of huevos rancheros and asked him what it was.

We took a cab back to the base. We passed the outer perimeter and its guard with no problem because the pilots had their Logair identification and I was in uniform. However, the flight line was on an inner perimeter and more difficult to enter. It had increased security because of the aircraft located there. We approached the gate with my father and the pilot discussing what to say to the guard to get me on the flight line. The pilot flashed on an idea. He told us, "We'll tell the guard that he's a courier." This was possible because I was in uniform.

So, all of a sudden, I became a Military Courier, carrying some undisclosed material or documents, I suppose.

The next stop on our flight west was Hill Air Force Base in Ogden, Utah. The night sky was very dark and overcast as we abruptly left the Wasatch Mountains behind and started our letdown for landing. The approach to Hill was completely on instruments with zero visibility. Sitting in the jump seat, I strained to see the runway lights, but saw nothing. I would have been concerned, except my father seemed confident as he went about his work. I'm sure he had been in this situation many times before, especially when flying over the Himalayas during the Second World War.

We were about 50 feet high when we broke out of the overcast. There, ahead, were the runway lights, laid out in front of us like parallel strings of pearls, but we weren't lined up with them; however, a quick dip of the wing straightened us out and we touched down just fine. My father had been flying the plane and I was very proud of his competence, brought about by many years of experience and training.

After Hill, we flew on to California. Sometime during the trip I had to use the restroom. When I asked where to go, the pilot and my father smiled at one another. I was instructed to work my way back past the cargo to the rear of the plane. When I got there I found a very smelly bucket that was used for this purpose. This definitely wasn't airline flying. Upon our arrival in California we landed at Travis Air Force Base in Fairfield. It was daylight by that time and my stepmother met us at the base and drove us home.

Home was 1404 Hurlbut Avenue in Sebastopol, California. In September my parents had moved from Belmont to a new house my father had built with some help from his Dad and a contractor neighbor. My father demonstrated his exceptional mechanical talents in building the house. He built the cabinetry, installed the plumbing and electrical, as well as put up the framing and sheet rock. After a belated and short, but very pleasant Christmas there, I found myself on another airline trip across country, back to Virginia Beach and the Guided Missile School.

Virginia Beach 1958-1959: white sand as far as the eye could see and a wide, gently sloping beach with old wooden, single-story hotels dotting the shore. A Coast Guard Station stood at the ready, its rescue lifeboats upside down on the shimmering sand, handy for any emergency. Scattered down the beach, an occasional dance hall stood ready to entertain the tourists. "3.2 beer" was served to those eighteen and older as they danced to the live music of Chubby Checker singing "The Twist" and, of course, there was also the requisite arcade found in any East Coast beach city.

The gentle waves of the deep-blue ocean slapped at the shoreline, as seagulls swooped and pelicans flew in formation down the beach. Water, almost as warm as a bath, invited all to dip their lily-white toes or to belly-surf on the incoming swells. In those pre-Civil Rights days, no "colored" people could be found anywhere near the beach. From place to place sand dunes rose, protecting young lovers as they sneaked a kiss or two. That was the ocean side of Atlantic Avenue.

The inland side of Atlantic Avenue was filled with stores dedicated to the tourists. Saltwater taffy shops placed their automatic taffy pulling machines out in front for all to see and to tempt the potential customer. Dozens of tee shirt and bathing suit shops, crammed side by side, lined the avenue. Dotted here and there were restaurants, but no chain restaurants. There weren't any fast-food chains at that time, but instead one-of-a-kind, family-owned restaurants like *Sambo's*. Of course, *Sambo's* was named after the story of "Little Black Sambo" in those days before racial enlightenment, with the Sambo story painted on the restaurant wall inside.

This was the Virginia Beach I was first introduced to in 1958: a small, East Coast beach town, shuttered in the winter when it was possible to find the sand dunes covered with snow. In the summer it was filled with college students. They came from the South, from as far west as Ohio, and as far north as New York. I had many good times in this picturesque little city and remember it with great fondness.

On January 3, 1959, Alaska became the 49th and largest state in the United States. Just a few months later, on August 21, Hawaii became the 50th state. That same year, the revolutionary leader, Fidel Castro, overthrew the dictator, Fulgencio Batista, to become premier of Cuba, which soon became allied with the USSR, establishing a Communist beachhead just ninety miles from the United States.

On March 13, I graduated from U.S. Naval Guided Missiles "A" School in Dam Neck, Virginia Beach, Virginia and was transferred to U.S. Naval Guided Missiles School at the General Dynamics Plant in Pomona, California where I attended Terrier surface-to-air Missile "C" School. In July I graduated from Terrier Missile School and was transferred to the USS *Norton Sound* (AVM-1) in Port Hueneme, California.

On September 17, the first rocket-powered flight of the North American X-15 was made. The X-15 was carried aloft attached to a modified B-52. On that flight it "only" reached Mach 2.3 in a shallow climb to 50,000 feet. Future flights would show it to be the fastest and highest-climbing aircraft ever built. Meanwhile, my father continued flying air force cargo for Resort Airlines.

Francis Gary Powers, a CIA pilot, flew the first Lockheed U-2 spy plane in 1956. On April 30, 1960, he was shot down over the Soviet Union while flying a U-2 on a spy mission. This quickly became a diplomatic disaster for almost everyone involved. The incident made President Eisenhower look like a liar and the Soviet leader, Nikita Khrushchev, look like a fool for trusting him. After that incident the U-2 continued to fly along the Iron Curtain, but supposedly never again deliberately penetrated Soviet airspace. Powers was put on trial in the Soviet Union, but was eventually allowed to return to the United States.

The world's first operational laser pulse was generated in May of 1960, ushering in one of the most important technological advances of the era, and NASA launched its first weather satellite.

John Fitzgerald Kennedy was elected as the 35th President of the United States in November of 1960. An inspiring public speaker, he promised to shake the country out of the lethargy of the Eisenhower years. His vision was a New Frontier of "uncharted areas of science and space . . . " Winning by a very slim margin, he became the nation's first Catholic president and its second youngest. It quickly became apparent this handsome New Englander was an energizing force for the entire country.

My father flew for Resort Airlines until June, when Resort lost its government Logair contract to World Airways, Inc. He was immediately hired to fly for World as a copilot on DC-4s out of Oakland, California. In December of 1960, Joe Goeller checked him out as a DC-4 captain. As captain, he continued to fly cargo around to Air Force bases throughout the United States, including Travis, Hill, Warner Robins, Charleston, Dover, Harrisburg, and San Antonio, among others.

Also in June, I was transferred back to the U.S. Naval Guided Missiles School in Pomona, California, for a Terrier BT-3 Refresher Course. "BT" described the Terrier missile's means of control (Beam Rider, Tail Control). In the prior course I had taken, the missile's means of control had been Beam Rider, Wing Control, or "BW." The "Beam" was a radar beam the missile rode up to the target.

I graduated on July 29 and was immediately transferred to the USS *Mahan* (DLG-11), a brand new Destroyer Leader, Guided Missile being built at Hunter's Point Naval Shipyard in San Francisco, California.

On April 12, 1961, a Soviet Cosmonaut named Yuri Gaga-
rin became the first man in space. He orbited Earth for eighty-
nine minutes in Vostok I. The newly inaugurated president,
John F. Kennedy, wasn't at all happy with this development.
The Soviet Union had sent the first animal into space and it
had again beaten the United States in the race to get a man
into space. Feeling that was enough, the President told Congress that America would be the first to land a man on the
moon. The space race was on.

On May 5, Alan B. Shepard, Jr. of Virginia Beach, Virginia
became the first American in space. His was a sub-orbital flight
aboard the first Mercury Project spacecraft. The excitement
resulting from this feat was somewhat dampened, however,
because the Soviets had been first and had stayed up longer.

My father's mother, Ann, was visiting my father in Sebastopol when she suddenly died from a heart attack. Born on
April 27, 1895, she was 66 years old. I was outside San Francisco's Golden Gate on the Destroyer Leader USS *Mahan* at the
time. The ship was out for the day on sea trials.

When we pulled into San Francisco and tied up to the
pier, one of my fellow sailors asked me how many days leave
I was taking. I told him I wasn't planning on taking any leave.
I soon found out what had happened to my grandmother and
that my stepmother had contacted the ship's Captain requesting I be allowed to attend my grandmother's funeral. Things
happened so quickly that this was all arranged without my
knowledge.

Chapter 15
DC-6A Captain

His second wife was gone
And he labored being free
But it wasn't very long before
He was caught by number three

In June 1961, my father began training in a DC-6A. He received his Federal Aviation Administration (FAA) type rating for that plane on June 23. Beginning in July, he began flying DC-6As as Captain.

Meanwhile, on August 13, Communist soldiers began building a 30-mile barrier of concrete block and barbed wire in East Germany. This highly visible manifestation of the Iron Curtain separated East Berlin from West Berlin. It became known as "the Berlin Wall" and stood for another 28 years.

The first flight of the predecessor of the Harrier vertical-takeoff-and-landing (VTOL) fighter-bomber took place on March 13, 1961. It was designated the P1127. Developed by the Bristol Company (which became Rolls-Royce) in Great Britain, it obtained vertical flight through thrust vectoring of its Pegasus jet engine; that is, the jet's thrust could be directed both downward and rearward through moveable ducts.

Also in 1961 the U.S. Air Force granted a contract to a consortium of companies consisting of LTV, Ryan, and the company for whom my father once worked, Hiller. The contract was for a VTOL transport based on Hiller's X18 and designated the XC-142. Only five planes and four engines were built. It was not mass-produced due to technical problems. The Air Force decided its Lockheed C-130 Hercules tactical transport was versatile enough to meet its requirements.

The Cold War heated to the boiling point in 1962 with the onset of the Cuban Missile Crisis. Nikita Khrushchev had ordered Soviet missiles to be quietly installed in Cuba. The two main reasons for doing this were to protect the USSR's Western Hemisphere ally from the United States, and as a response to the U.S. placing its own missiles in Turkey.

A U-2 aircraft first photographed the Cuban installations on October 14. President Kennedy was stunned and at first kept the fact quiet; however, a week later, he announced the crisis to an equally shocked America. For thirteen days in October the United States and the Soviet Union were locked in an atomic face-off. To everyone's relief, on October 28 Khrushchev backed down and started shipping the missiles back to the Soviet Union. Later, the U.S. began removing its own missiles from Turkey.

On a more personal note, my relationship with my stepmother was often strained as I was growing up. I felt she was too strict with me as I was going through high school. In my senior year I asked to be able to attend college away from home so I could be on my own. This request was denied, most likely for financial reasons, so I attended a local junior college for a while.

I had more or less floated through a couple of semesters of college without really knowing what I wanted to do with my life. At the same time I felt my stepmother was too intrusive in my post-high school life. Therefore, in my second semester, I stopped even the minimal effort I was putting into school and joined the Navy.

After my first enlistment was over, I lived in Southern California. I made one trip to my parents' house during that time. I spent the afternoon talking with my stepmother outside on the patio. My father was home, but had just returned from one of his trips flying around the country and I was told not to disturb him. Once again, circumstances were keeping me away from my father. I continued finding it very difficult to have a close relationship with a father who was gone so much.

I was discharged from the Navy on March 20, 1962, and had been working at rather mediocre jobs in the Los Angeles area when the Cuban Missile Crisis occurred. One day I happened to be at the harbor in Los Angeles and noticed all the Navy ships were gone and the strangest feeling came over me. I had just spent four years training in the Navy and now that the Navy was embroiled in an international incident, I wasn't involved.

This started me thinking about rejoining. I thought if I went back and really applied myself in the Navy's schools I knew I would be able to attend, I could come out better qualified to get a decent job. I visited a recruiter and told him if I could get into submarine school, I would re-enlist. The recruiter arranged it and in November I was back in the Navy. I drove across country to New London, Connecticut where I attended submarine school. It was quite some time before I saw my father again.

On February 28, 1962, Lt. Col. John Glenn became the first American to orbit the earth. His Mercury capsule, *Friendship 7*, was the first to be lifted into space atop an Atlas Intercontinental Ballistic Missile. The Atlas was powerful enough to boost Glenn into earth orbit. Also in 1962, the *Mariner 2* spacecraft identified the presence of "solar wind" in the universe. Solar wind is essentially energetic bursts of atoms, ions, and electrons emitted by activity on the sun.

On November 29, 1962, two essential agreements were signed specifying that the British and French governments would put up the money and four British and French companies would jointly develop the engines and airframe for what would be the world's first successful supersonic transport airplane. The result of that combined effort was aptly named the Concorde.

My father continued flying for World Airways in 1962 and 1963. I was once again all the way across country from him. While he was flying piston-engine planes, one of the great successes in the history of commercial aircraft was flown for the first time. The Boeing 727 short-to-medium range jet airliner made its debut in February 1963 and is still flown today by some of the world's major airlines. It was America's first certified, commercial tri-jet.

I graduated from U.S. Naval Submarine School on January 30, 1963 and was again transferred to the United States Naval Guided Missiles School in Dam Neck, Virginia Beach, Virginia. For a very short period of time between Submarine School and Guided Missile School, I was temporarily stationed on an old World War II Submarine, the USS *Cubera* (SS-347). While stationed on the *Cubera* out of Norfolk, Virginia, I visited the fast attack Submarine USS *Scorpion* (SSN-589) with a shipmate who had a friend on that boat. Compared to the WWII vintage boat we were on, the Scorpion was very modern.

I heard the news on April 10, 1963 that the USS *Thresher* (SSN-593), a nuclear-powered attack submarine going through sea trials out of Portsmouth, New Hampshire, failed during a test dive. It fell to the sea bottom 1,300 feet below, with a loss of 129 men. To someone just entering the submarine service, this made me stop and think about what I was getting myself into. But at that age, I didn't think something like that would ever happen to me.

The American Mercury Project had come to a successful conclusion in May 1963 with the 22-orbit, 34-hour flight of L.

Gordon Cooper. At age 36, he was the youngest of the "original seven" American astronauts. After six manned voyages, Mercury had served its purpose: Americans had gone into space and survived. However, in June 1963, the Soviets expanded their lead in space by sending the first woman into orbit. She was Cosmonaut Valentina V. Tereshkova aboard *Vostok 6.*

During the summer, while attending Guided Missile School in Virginia Beach, I met a young woman from North Carolina. During the school year she attended the University of North Carolina Women's College in Greensboro. We started dating and just ten weeks after we met, on November 8, 1963, I married Alice Louise Isley of Ramseur, North Carolina.

Any American old enough to remember November 22, 1963, knows exactly what he or she was doing when the announcement was made that President John F. Kennedy had been shot. The man who had made many Americans proud of their country, whose term in office was likened to Camelot, lay critically wounded. I was driving between Virginia Beach, Virginia and Ramseur, North Carolina to spend a belated honeymoon with my new wife. Just as I was about to cross the state line the announcement came over the car radio that something had happened to the President. Radio reception wasn't very good at that point and I strained to learn exactly what was going on.

After crossing the state line, I stopped at a liquor store and the person working there had a transistor radio sitting on top of the counter, tuned to the news. That's when I learned exactly what had happened—the President had been shot while riding in a motorcade in Dallas, Texas. It wasn't immediately known whether or not he had been killed, so I joined the millions of Americans praying for a miracle as I continued on to Ramseur. Of course, everyone soon learned the worst—President Kennedy was dead and Vice President Lyndon B. Johnson had been sworn in as the new President of the United

States. I spent most of my honeymoon in front of the television watching the events unfold in Texas.

Upon graduation from Guided Missile School, I was transferred to the Polaris Nuclear Missile Submarine USS *James Monroe* (SSBN 622), reporting aboard December 3, 1963. The *James Monroe* was located at the Newport News Naval Shipyard in Virginia. She was a new sub getting her final fitting out prior to sea trials. While aboard, I received a letter from my parents back in California telling me they were getting a divorce. I was shocked, surprised, and very upset by this news. I hadn't seen it coming.

I had left home to get away from a stepmother who I felt was too strict, but though she was strict, she had provided stability in my life. Living on my own and getting married had given me a sense of self-confidence I never before had. With self-confidence came a mature state of mind from which I could see my stepmother in a more positive light. She'd taught me many things. She introduced me to new ideas. She had been there for me. But more than that, for the first time since my real mother had died when I was nine, she'd given me a solid footing in life, a rooted foundation from which to grow. Now I was afraid that foundation was being taken away.

I panicked and requested emergency leave. Because a submarine's Executive Officer is primarily in charge of personnel matters, our ship's Exec called me in to talk about my request. I showed him my parent's letter and he read it carefully. He then asked, "What do you expect to do if I approve your leave?" I told him I wanted to go home and try to patch things up between my parents.

He explained to me the letter showed both my parents had thought things through very thoroughly and seemed confident they were making the right decision. My going to California to try and alter things would only add complexity to the situation without really changing anything. He convinced me the divorce was real and I would have to accept it. I believed what he told me and followed his advice. Their divorce became final on March 6, 1964.

My stepmother initiated my parent's divorce. Years later I asked her why she left my father. Initially she would only say she and my father were not compatible. When I questioned her further, the fact emerged I wasn't the only one who felt a distance from my father. It seems when he went off on his own, flying, he left both my stepmother and me to make it on our own. After I joined the Navy, he continued leaving my stepmother to fend for herself. We both felt the distance, but she didn't have to live with it like I did. Another aspect of the relationship was that my stepmother felt my father was "living his former life" to some extent. In other words, deep down, he felt my mother, Mercedes, was his one true love and this affected his interaction with Evelyn.

Immediately after the divorce, Thelma Maurine McDonald of Sebastopol began pursuing my father. She attended the same Episcopal Church as my father and stepmother. Thelma first asked my stepmother if there was any chance for reconciliation. When Evelyn told her there wasn't, she pounced. My father was the kind of person who was heavily influenced by women. He needed to have a female partner in his life. That made him vulnerable to Thelma's advances and on June 22, 1964, he remarried, moving in with Thelma at 7308 Bodega Avenue in Sebastopol. He remained flying as Captain on DC-6As for World Airways and I maintained my relationship with my stepmother, Evelyn.

The NASA Gemini Project was the logical follow-up to the Mercury Project. Its purpose was to subject two men and their supporting equipment to long-duration space flight. The first two Gemini flights were unmanned tests of both the more powerful Titan 2 military missile and the Gemini spacecraft itself. *Gemini 1* was launched into orbit on April 8, 1964. No attempt was made to return and recover the spacecraft.

The Gulf of Tonkin Resolution gave President Lyndon Johnson broad powers to wage an undeclared war in Vietnam without the normal Congressional checks and balances. His use of that power triggered a rash of anti-war demonstrations and loss of Congressional allies, especially because the justification for the resolution was shaky. American ships had been patrolling the Gulf of Tonkin for the South Vietnamese during the summer of 1964. On August 2, U.S. officials reported the North Vietnamese, without provocation, had attacked the USS *Maddox*. Two days later, the *Maddox* and the USS *Turner Joy* reported more unprovoked fire. News later leaked out the first attack was not unprovoked and the second probably never happened. Johnson supporters felt duped.

The USS *James Monroe*'s crews had relocated to Charleston, South Carolina, while the submarine itself was operating out of Rota, Spain. The Gold crew had taken the sub over to Spain and gone on the first patrol with her. I was on the Blue crew, which would relieve the Gold crew and take the boat out for its second patrol. In the fall, after one patrol, I became qualified in submarines. This allowed me to wear the "Dolphins" which are the official insignia of the Navy's submariners.

Lockheed Aircraft's SR-71 Blackbird, the first Mach 3 airplane to enter service with the U.S. Air Force, first flew in December 1964. This was the ultimate high-performance strategic reconnaissance aircraft. Also in 1964, Geraldine Mock of West Germany became the first woman to fly around the world solo.

In 1965, America's involvement in Vietnam deepened when President Johnson dispatched two Marine battalions to protect an air base at Da Nang. These were combat soldiers, unlike the 23,500 troops already there, and designated "advisers."

After one patrol on the USS *James Monroe* I "de-volunteered" from submarines in order to have more time with my new wife. As a result, I was transferred to the USS *Simon Lake* (AS-33) in January 1965. The *Simon Lake* was a submarine tender being placed in commission in Bremerton, Washington.

After sea trials, the *Simon Lake* sailed through the Panama Canal to reach its new homeport of Charleston, South Carolina. Instead of going from the West Coast to the East Coast with the ship, my wife and I drove across country with another couple from the ship. It was quite a trip with four people in a small, white Corvair, pulling a single-wheeled trailer across the northern tier of states in winter.

After arriving in Charleston, my wife and I rented a trailer in a small mobile home park on Montague in North Charleston. The address was Route 2, Box 583, Charleston Heights, South Carolina. One of my father's stops, as he flew air force cargo around the U.S. for World Airways, was Charleston Air Force Base. I was very excited when I learned he was going to make a stop in Charleston. It had been quite a while since I had seen him, inasmuch as we were living on opposite coasts from one another.

Because of my father's recent marriage, my wife and I went to the Base Exchange to find a wedding gift for him and his new bride. We picked out a large wall clock that had a round, golden clock assembly, a white face with black numbers, and wooden spokes radiating out from the center face. When it was time for him to land, we rushed out to the Air Base in our little brown 1962 Corvair to meet him.

We brought him to our mobile home, gave him his gift and showed him our new 14-foot runabout outboard motorboat. He seemed genuinely interested in me and seemed happy to see me, which made me feel good. He even took my wife and me out to the flight line and gave us a tour of his plane. It's normally very difficult to go near the flight line of an Air Force base, but he managed it. By the time we toured his plane it was nightfall and the plane's interior was dark, but I was in seventh heaven, having my father show me all about his DC-6A. It wasn't that it was new to me, but having my father spend time sharing his world with me was very, very special.

A second unmanned Gemini flight in January 1965 successfully demonstrated the vehicle's ability to withstand the heat and stress of re-entry into the Earth's atmosphere. Then, on March 18, Soviet cosmonaut Aleksei Leonov became the first man to walk in space from the two-man *Voskhod 2* spacecraft and on March 23, *Gemini 3* was launched with two astronauts aboard. It became the first spacecraft, American or Soviet, to change the plane and size of its Earth orbit. With this flight, the Gemini spacecraft was deemed flight worthy, so NASA went ahead with nine more of the two-man missions over the next eighteen months.

A little over a year after its first flight, Lockheed Aircraft's SR-71 Blackbird entered service in January 1966. Above and beyond the reach of winged aircraft, progress in space accelerated this year. In February, the Soviet Union's *Luna 9* made the first soft landing on the moon, returning photographs of the lunar surface. In March, the Soviet's *Luna 10* became the first spacecraft to orbit the moon. The United States soft-landed its *Surveyor 1* on the moon's surface in May followed by its *Lunar Orbiter 1*, which began circling the moon on August 10.

On February 26, 1966, NASA made the first full-scale, unmanned test of an Apollo spacecraft. The Apollo program was America's project for sending a man to the moon and safely returning him to Earth. This first test consisted of a Command Module and a Service Module. Fired 5,500 miles down the Atlantic Missile Range by a Saturn 1-B rocket, the flight was rated as "a successful first step" by Apollo officials.

Chapter 16
A Cessna of His Own

A wish had come true
He owned his own plane
But as happens in life
Pleasure is tempered by pain

Developments in the aerospace industry had pushed the envelope so men could fly faster and higher than ever before. Although my father was still flying piston aircraft for World Airways, 1966 was a special year for him because he purchased his own airplane. It was a Cessna 182A, I.D. Number 5056D. He took his first trip in it on March 27, 1966, flying to Tahoe and Reno then returning to Santa Rosa Airport. After a few more short hops, he flew cross-country to Ogden, Utah. On both the outbound and return legs, he stopped in Reno and Elko, Nevada.

I had no idea my father had purchased an airplane until much later. I was living on the East Coast at the time and that little piece of information just wasn't received. I'm not sure whether my father just failed to tell me, or if it was because I was too wrapped up in my own life to notice.

In July, the USS *Simon Lake*, on which I was stationed,

transferred to Holy Loch, Scotland. I went with the ship to Scotland where I was re-assigned to the USS *Hunley* (AS-31). The *Hunley* was the submarine tender relieved by the *Simon Lake*. I was transferred to the *Hunley* because my second Navy enlistment was about to end.

The *Hunley* returned to Charleston, South Carolina via Lisbon, Portugal. It was quite a change going from the cold weather of Scotland to the oppressive heat of Portugal. In Scotland we wore our Navy peacoats most of the time. In Portugal, I went ashore to look around Lisbon, but had to return to the ship because of an extremely bad headache. The blazing sun and the beer apparently didn't mix well.

On November 18, I was discharged from the Navy. That same month, some students began burning their draft cards in protest against the Vietnam War draft. The number of men being drafted had doubled in the last year. Having just spent eight years of my life in the military, I thought the students were all a bunch of un-American "crazies." My father had gone to war in Burma to defend world democracy. I didn't understand just how different the situation was between the Vietnam War and the Second World War.

I'd grown up in the Navy. It took me two four-year enlistments to do it, but it finally worked. I first entered the Navy as a 19-year-old with an immature and wandering soul. I emerged eight years later as a mature, married person prepared for a career in electronics. When I first entered the Service I had no idea what I wanted to do with my life—that's one reason why I quit college and enlisted. The Navy gave me a battery of tests to see where I might best succeed. It turned out that I did well enough to attend school in what was then the new and emerging field of guided missiles.

Learning about guided missiles meant learning electronics. Initially, I was taught all about vacuum tubes. I soon learned, however, there were no vacuum tubes in naval guided missiles. Therefore, I was quickly introduced to the world of semi-conductors. In 1966, not many people, including me, had any idea what a semiconductor was. I soon gained a skill that prepared me for a professional career.

Why didn't I know what I wanted to do with my life? Today you see kids with clear understandings of what their passions are, what they want to do with their lives. I believe the difference between them and me is they were raised in a reasonably stable world. I was born the year World War II began. My father, being a pilot and then in the Army Air Force, moved around a lot and, of course, that affected me. After the war was over and my mother died, I was moved around even more. I ended up attending 22 schools before reaching high school. I was lucky if I knew what day it was, much less what I wanted to do with my life.

After my discharge, my wife and I drove across the country from Charleston, South Carolina to Anaheim, California in our first new car. It was a yellow 1965 Corvair. Fortunately, the Northrop "tech rep" onboard the *Simon Lake* had given me a letter of recommendation to present to the hiring manager at his company. I was greatly relieved because this made my job search very simple. Thanks to that letter, I got a job at the Nortronics Division of Northrop Corporation in Anaheim, California. Northrop made test-and-readiness equipment for Polaris submarines. With employment taken care of, my wife and I moved into a small one-bedroom apartment on Lincoln Avenue in Anaheim, California.

On January 27, 1967, preparations were underway for the first manned flight of an Apollo spacecraft. With three fully-suited astronauts lying strapped in the seats of *Apollo I* and the hatch closed and sealed, one of the crew suddenly reported a fire inside the capsule. A sharp cry of pain was heard, then silence. NASA calculated that in less than a minute all three astronauts lost consciousness. Because there was no emergency hatch release, they were trapped inside and beyond rescue in less than four minutes. This tragedy delayed the Apollo project for about a year and a half, but the project did proceed. As one of the dead astronauts had said earlier, "If we die, we want people to accept it. We are in a risky business."

The Boeing 737-200 made its maiden flight in August 1967. Production had begun in 1966. Lufthansa German Airlines was the launch customer, ordering twenty-one 737-100s, making it the only Boeing airliner sold to a foreign buyer before an American purchase was made. Over 1,000 Model 200-737's were built before production was ended 22 years later. Meanwhile, my father continued flying DC-6As for World Airways. He also enjoyed flying his new Cessna between his professional trips around the country.

In June 1967, the 19-year-old state of Israel quadrupled its size. Since the mid-1950s, displaced Palestinians and other Arabs had been skirmishing with Israel along its borders with Lebanon, Syria, and Jordan. The fighting escalated that year when Egypt sent troops to Israel's southern border on the Sinai Peninsula and blockaded the Strait of Tiran. In what was to become known as the "Six-Day War," Israel crushed a multinational Arabic army in just that many days. It was a stunning victory for the Jewish state, but it laid the groundwork for decades of strife in the region.

I was just vaguely aware of these events as I began attending classes at Fullerton Junior College. I was working full-time at Northrop and going to school at night. My focus was earning a two-year degree in Electronic Engineering, learning a new job, and setting up a new household. To enhance the latter, we moved into a larger, two-bedroom apartment in the same complex where we were living on Lincoln Avenue in Anaheim.

On January 31, 1968, North Vietnamese guerrillas broke a truce with the South Vietnamese and attacked several targets in the south. Known as the "Tet Offensive" (because it occurred during Vietnam's traditional New Year's celebration, "Tet"), this action caused more casualties in one month than ever before in the war. As a result, the growing antiwar protests in the United States reached an all-time high. People of all ages and backgrounds took part in the demonstrations.

On March 16 in Vietnam, a platoon of American infantrymen stormed the village of My Lai near the South Vietnamese coast. It was thought to be home to Viet Cong sympathizers. The troops' purpose was to rid the village of the enemy; however, they found only unarmed women, children and old men. Despite this, the villagers were rounded up and more than 300 were massacred. The angry GIs were out to seek vengeance for their fallen comrades in arms.

President Lyndon Baines Johnson, like President Harry S. Truman before him, was tied down with an "unwinnable" war. This time it was in Vietnam. History repeated itself when Johnson, like Truman, announced he would not seek re-election. Richard M. Nixon was elected President in 1968 by Americans tired of Vietnam, but uncomfortable with defeat. Nixon's catch phrase "peace with honor" went over well with the general public.

On May 27, 1968, the submarine USS *Scorpion* (SSN-589) was reported missing. This was the same boat I had visited while stationed on a submarine in Virginia back in 1963. On June 5, the Navy announced the *Scorpion* was lost along with 99 officers and men. This brought home the message that my Executive Officer on the USS *James Monroe* had given me: Submarines are very dangerous and everyone aboard needs to know exactly what they are doing at all times. With the loss of both the *Thresher* and the *Scorpion*, I felt very fortunate to be alive.

On September 30, 1968, the first "wide body" aircraft, the Boeing 747 Superjet, made its world debut in a roll-out ceremony in Everett, Washington.

Later that year I remember taking an after-dinner walk with my Uncle Russ and my father in front of my uncle's house. It was the first time I had seen my uncle in a long time. I knew he had suffered a heart attack earlier, but he seemed fully recovered and quite at ease. He told my father and me about how he felt as the ambulance pulled away from his house while he lay in the back. He said, "I said to myself, *I can't go yet. I have too many things to take care of first.*" After he recovered, he took care of all the loose ends he needed to do for his family's sake. To my surprise, he said, "Now I'm ready. I can go any time."

I more or less placed little stock in his statement at the time. I was just enjoying walking and talking with my father and my uncle. They treated me as an equal, as an adult, which, of course, I was, but it was the first time I had ever had that feeling with my father. My father and his brother had always been close and at long last, I was included in their circle of camaraderie. My Uncle Russ was born Russell Chastain—no middle name—in 1918 during the worldwide flu epidemic. My father, five years old at the time, had helped his mother heat barley water for Russell because both of my grandparents were down with the flu. My father didn't burn down the house as my grandmother had feared, but a bond had been formed between him and his baby brother.

During World War II, when Uncle Russ enlisted in the Navy, he was asked what his middle initial was. He answered he didn't have one. He was told he had to have one. "After all, didn't everybody?" My grandmother Ann was with him and told the Navy recruiter his middle initial was "H." She later told me she just made it up on the spot because the Navy insisted he at least have a middle initial. From then on he was Russell H. Chastain.

After our walk, my uncle, my father and I went back into the house and once again mixed with the rest of the family.

The special moment had passed. It wasn't long after that when Uncle Russ died. Born on August 31, 1918, in Deming, New Mexico, he died on August 30, 1968. He was just one day short of his 50th birthday when a second heart attack took him away. It was sad to see him die at such a young age, but, as he had told my father and me during that special walk not long before, he was ready.

For most of 1968 my father lived in Sebastopol, working for World Airways and flying his Cessna for pleasure when time allowed. For World, he had made flights to Kwajalein Island in the Pacific Ocean. Those flights were part of the Nike-X (Missile) Olympian Service. He received a certificate for the "Last Flight from Kwajalein" on September 28, 1968.

In December, World Airways transferred him to San Antonio, Texas to operate out of Kelly Air Force Base. The night before they left for San Antonio, the Sebastopol house he and his wife Thelma had been renting burned down. The movers had come in and packed up everything to be picked up the next day, so my father and Thelma spent the night in a motel. Because they weren't going to be in the house overnight, my father turned the heater down. Unfortunately, apparently there was a gas leak in the heater. Because it had been turned down, enough time elapsed for gas to accumulate before the heater came on. When it did, it exploded, starting a fire that destroyed much of my father's belongings.

My father lost a valuable coin collection, which, ironically, had been stored above the heater, as well as a significant set of bound *National Geographic* magazines he had gotten from his father, Everett. He also lost some World War II memorabilia. Raised during the Great Depression and having very little in material possessions as he was growing up, my father didn't dwell on his misfortune. He picked up, moved to San Antonio and went on with his life. In San Antonio, he and Thelma lived in an apartment at 1000 Jackson Keller Road. He put his

Cessna in storage at Santa Rosa Airport in California while they lived in Texas.

The Apollo program got back on track in 1968. On October 11, *Apollo 7*, with its three-man crew, became the first manned flight of the spacecraft. Then on December 21, *Apollo 8* was launched. That craft and its crew made the first manned orbit of the moon. No one had ever ventured beyond Earth's orbit before, but this awesome mission was accomplished without a hitch.

On February 9, 1969, the Boeing Airplane Company's new 747 made its maiden flight. At the time, the 747 was the largest civilian transport aircraft in the world. The age of the jumbo jet had arrived. The 747 was FAA certified on December 30 of the same year. That behemoth revolutionized the air transport business. With a maximum speed of 610 miles per hour, the 747-200 carried up to 442 passengers.

Not to be outdone, Lockheed's C-5A Galaxy long-range logistics transport entered service with the U.S. Air Force's Military Airlift Command (MAC) that same year. Over 247 feet long, with a wingspan of over 222 feet and four jet engines, the C5-A was a giant step above the C-47 Skytrains my father flew when flying for World War II's version of MAC, the Air Transport Command (ATC).

On July 20, 1969, the world sat spellbound in front of televisions and radios, as an American astronaut became the first man to set foot on the moon. Neil Armstrong, and then Buzz Aldrin, hopped about like kangaroos in the weak lunar gravity. The late President Kennedy's proclamation had come to pass. Preceded by *Apollo 9* in March and *Apollo 10* in May, *Apollo 11* had taken men to the moon's surface and returned them safely to the earth. The total time spent on the moon by Armstrong and Aldrin was 21½ hours. During that time the lunar surface had been permanently changed. Besides the American flag, the first human footprints were left behind in the dust.

The world's first vertical takeoff and landing (VTOL) strike and reconnaissance fighter, the Harrier, entered squadron service with Britain's Royal Air Force (RAF) in June 1969. Four rotatable nozzles, two on each side, achieve vertical lift. The nozzles point down for lift and are then gradually rotated rearward to provide forward propulsion. The U.S. Marine Corps ordered some of those aircraft in September.

Kenneth with his Cessna 182, I.D. 5056D (1966)

Chapter 17
Jets

He was young, barely formed
As were the planes he would fly
He and aviation grew together
Until the day it passed him by

My father took up flying in an age when aviation was a new and very dangerous thing to do. He soloed in an extremely rudimentary airplane, a plane that eventually lost a wing in flight, killing its pilot. As my father grew and matured, so did aviation. When he flew during World War II, he took the controls of that era's most sophisticated bombers and cargo aircraft. He flew C47s beyond the limit of their design specifications at the top of the world—the Himalayas. After the war he continued flying in propeller-driven transports until they were finally phased out of service.

In July 1969, World Airways transferred my father back to the San Francisco Bay Area to undergo jet training. World was no longer going to use propeller aircraft in its operations. He and Thelma moved into an apartment at 1300 Creekside Drive in Walnut Creek. In August, after undergoing cockpit procedures training and Boeing 720 simulator training in

Denver, Colorado, he began flight training in a Boeing 707 out of Oakland. After nine hours and forty-five minutes of flight training, my father was terminated because of his difficulty transitioning to jets. His last professional flight was in a Boeing 707 on September 24, 1969. For reasons I don't know or understand, he also sold his Cessna—perhaps he had just had enough of flying at that point in his life.

Aviation development had finally passed him by. Born a mere ten years after man flew powered aircraft for the first time, his life had paralleled the development of aviation, all the way up to the Space Age. The year my father made his last professional flight was the year man landed on the moon and the year the Boeing 747 and the Lockheed C5A made their debut. After 37 years of flying, he retired at a very appropriate time. The baton had been passed to the Jet and Space Age generation.

On November 22, 1969, my father's only grandchild was born. While we were at the hospital, the crew of *Apollo 12* was shown on television. After making man's second trip to the moon, the astronauts were being recovered from their space capsule *Yankee Clipper* after splashdown in the Pacific Ocean. My daughter, Shauna Lynn Chastain, was born in Anaheim, California that day. My father had entered the final stage of his life and a new generation had come into the world.

EPILOGUE

My father spent 37 years of his life in aviation. After retiring from flying and selling his Cessna, he purchased a mobile home located at 140 Tiffany Drive in Santa Rosa, California. He moved in with his third wife, Thelma, and lived there for 25 years. Between 1970 and 1972, the Apollo space program launched five more spacecraft to the moon. With the notable exception of *Apollo 13*, all ended with more men landing on the moon and returning safely to the earth. *Apollo 13* had an oxygen generator blow up while in space. Fortunately, the explosion was not fatal and NASA successfully recovered the astronauts. *Apollo 17* was the final mission and marked the last time man would venture to the moon in my father's lifetime.

In 1972, after a two-year hiatus from airplanes and flying, my father decided to get involved once again. He took a position as Aviation Parts Manager for Redwood Aviation in Santa Rosa. He also began flying again. The last plane he had flown was a Boeing 707 back in 1969 when he failed to transition to jets. He now flew Redwood Aviation's Piper PA-22 Tri-pacer for his own pleasure. His resumption of flying coincided with the founding of Federal Express, a new airline with the unique idea of transporting packages around the country, rather than passengers.

In the wake of a rash of airborne terrorism, airports in the United States began inspecting luggage and passengers in 1973. This new twist to air transportation was never envisioned by the pioneers of aviation as they struggled to make flying safe, but that same year, my father was quite safe as he flew Redwood Aviation's Piper PA28-140 Cherokee. As with other modern aircraft, the Cherokee benefited from the work begun in 1928 when the first Aeronautical Safety Conference was held, sponsored by the Daniel Guggenheim Fund for Promotion of Aeronautics. Soon after that, the Guggenheim Fund began awarding $100,000 prizes for significant safety improvements through its annual safe aircraft competition.

In 1974, besides flying the company's Piper Cherokees, my father also flew a Piper Seneca; however, that year would mark his last flight for ten years when he made a thirty-minute pleasure flight in an open cockpit biplane—a Great Lakes. He had last flown a Great Lakes in 1936 when he flew in one to the Air Races at Mines Field in Los Angeles (now LAX).

A joint U.S. and USSR Apollo-Soyuz space mission docked in orbit in 1975. This cooperative effort by marginal enemies transformed the exploration of space from a frantic race into a venture that promised the mutually beneficial exchange of technology. As the U.S. and the Soviet Union came closer together in space, my father, then 62, and of retirement age, again left the employ of aviation and stopped working for Redwood Aviation. Although he was in full retirement, he never completely abandoned airplanes. He spent much of his spare time doing what he had done off and on most of his life: building model planes.

Two years after his retirement, two Boeing 747s collided on a runway at Tenerife, Canary Islands. Five hundred and seventy-four people were killed, making it the worst accident in aviation history. Also in 1977, my father joined the Hump Pilot's Association (HPA). The HPA was an organization founded to gather former Hump Pilots together to preserve the comradeship they forged in the storms above the mountains of Burma and China during World War II.

The theatre of war was known as China, Burma, India (CBI). In that time and place, Allied airmen took part in establishing for all time the truth that any machinery necessary to wage modern war could be airlifted from any place to any other place regardless of weather or terrain. These were the men of the Himalayas—the mighty Hump—and my father was one of those men.

On November 23, 1980, my grandfather, Everett Lee Chastain, passed away at the age of 88. He was born in the 19th Century on March 20, 1892, in Tahlequah, Oklahoma. When Everett was born, Oklahoma was not a state and was called "Indian Territory." Everett's father was Jefferson Davis Chastain. He was named after the President of the Confederate States of America. Everett's middle name, Lee, was given to him in honor of the great Southern General, Robert E. Lee. The name "Lee" was passed down to both my father and me.

Needless to say, the Chastains originated in the South, beginning with the French doctor, Pierre Chastain. He was given land in Virginia and settled there in the beginning of the 1700s. Over the years, the Chastains migrated first south to Georgia, then westward. Our branch of the family settled in California when Everett moved there before my father was born.

Everett lived through the bad times of the Great Depression, always finding work somewhere, somehow. Although poor during those years, he managed to find ways to care for his family. As previously mentioned, he survived the Japanese attack on Pearl Harbor, even though he worked as a carpenter at Ford Island at the time. Fortunately for him, the attack occurred on a Sunday when he wasn't at work, but he had watched as Japanese planes strafed and bombed his neighborhood.

Through his carpentry skills, Everett worked his way up to a comfortable life in Southern California. He built new homes for returning World War II veterans. He also purchased older homes and fixed them up for resale at a profit. Some of my grandfather's traits were passed on to my father. For instance, he had a very corny sense of humor and loved a pun. I remember him asking me one time what those heavy metal vehicles were that had tracks instead of wheels and a large protruding gun. I answered, "Tanks." He responded, "You're welcome." My father and I both inherited this slant on the droll.

Everett was obviously very resourceful and handy. In that regard, my father was just like him. While Everett was working hard to support his family, my father, being the oldest of four children, took responsibility for his siblings. That, and following his father's example, helped my father become a serious-minded person, but his responsible nature didn't interfere with his sense of humor. My grandfather may have left this earth, but his imprint was left on my father, and to some extent, on me.

My father was retired from flying, but advancements in aerospace continued unabated. On April 12, 1981, NASA launched the space shuttle *Columbia*. *Columbia* was the world's first reusable space vehicle. It orbited the earth thirty-six times, landing two days later.

Also in 1981, my father became more deeply committed to the HPA. He applied for and received lifetime membership (Membership Number 440).

Nineteen eighty-one wasn't the best year for me. After seventeen years of marriage, my wife, Alice, and I separated and eventually divorced. Breakups are always hard. Ours was extremely difficult. After such a long-term marriage, separation is a wrenching tear, rather than a clean break. It was very ugly by the time it was over. Fortunately, my stepmother gave me a lot of support during the divorce proceedings. Unfortunately, I didn't receive much support from my father, but it wasn't his fault.

My father's third wife, Thelma, had a way of making me feel unwelcome whenever I would visit. As a result, my visits tapered off to almost none. Once again a barrier had been placed between my father and me. By that time I had reached the conclusion I would never have a close relationship with my father in my lifetime. It was a struggle reaching that conclusion, but I couldn't go on always feeling cheated. I felt cheated by my mother's premature death and I felt cheated by the constant emotional distance between my father and me. Although I loved my father very much, love didn't seem to be enough. Reality was a different thing.

In 1984 it had been ten years since my father last flew an airplane, but on July 5, 1984, he flew a Piper PA-28-161 Cherokee for a biannual flight check. On July 13, he made his last private flight in another Piper Cherokee. The flight lasted forty-two minutes. Flying was now a thing of his past.

As with President Kennedy's assassination, most people can recall where they were on January 28, 1986, when the space shuttle *Challenger* exploded during launch. All seven people on board were killed. Besides astronauts, the crew included Christa McAuliffe, a Concord, New Hampshire schoolteacher. Christa had been selected to be the first person to teach classes from space. It was a tragic and eye-opening moment for all of the schoolchildren watching as the liftoff went terribly wrong. Once again, fate reminded the world that flying in space is a dangerous endeavor.

On December 21, 1988, the world was reminded that flying closer to the earth can be just as dangerous as space flight when international terrorism intervenes. On that date, Pan American Airlines Flight 103 exploded in midair six miles above Lockerbie, Scotland. The Boeing 747 was carrying 259 passengers when it went down, killing all aboard. Middle Eastern terrorist groups claimed responsibility for the appalling act.

The last year of the decade of the Eighties became another watershed year for both the world and for my father. In that year the Soviet Union lost its grip on Eastern Europe and the Iron Curtain came crashing down. The fall of Eastern European Communism was vividly symbolized by the sudden destruction of the Berlin Wall. In that same year, my father's third wife passed away. After each of these events, nothing was quite the same.

My father started visiting me a lot more often after Thelma died, but even though I was now seeing more of him, there remained a distance between us. The distance was barely perceptible, but it was there. I had remarried in 1983. My new wife, Juliette, and my father got along well. Juliette was a trained social worker and very intuitive when it came to people.

It wasn't long before she felt the distance between my father and me. She assumed the problem was the fact my father and I had just not spent a lot of time together for many, many years. One day Juliette, my father and I were standing by my father's car saying goodbye after one of his visits. I started to shake his hand, as was our custom, when Juliette pushed us together and said, "For goodness sake, hug one another." We did. That simple but perceptive act by Juliette brought my father and me closer than I had ever imagined possible.

In September 1990, my father attended a Hump Pilot's reunion in Virginia Beach, Virginia. By a stroke of good fortune, I was also on the East Coast attending a business conference in Washington, D.C. Because we were in the same part of the country at the same time, my father and I decided to meet in Virginia Beach after his meeting was over. Once together, we set out to explore Jamestown, Williamsburg, and Manakin, Virginia.

Manakin is a one-gas-station town outside Richmond, Virginia. My father's interest in genealogy had led him to discover that he and I are descendants of the French Huguenot refugee, Dr. Pierre Chastain. Dr. Chastain and his family had settled in the Manakin area after arriving in Jamestown, Virginia, aboard the ship *Mary and Ann* on July 23, 1700. Because the Chastains were Huguenots (or Protestants) in the very Catholic country of France, they suffered religious persecution and threat of death. To ensure the family's survival, they fled the ancient French Province of Berri (now the Department of Cher) in central France, and ended up in England.

The King of England granted many French Huguenot refugees land in Virginia. Once there, the refugees were expected to provide for themselves. Each family had to build their own shelter. There was little or no food, clothing, or stoves for warmth. The land they settled on had belonged to Indians known to kill settlers. The hardships they endured took their toll on Dr. Chastain's first wife. She died not long after they arrived in America. The following year three of their children also died. Nevertheless, the resilient Dr. Pierre Chastain remarried and had more children, thus ensuring the family's survival in a harsh, new land.

In Manakin, we first searched for the old Huguenot Church, then for the grave of Pierre Chastain. The original church used by the Huguenots in the early 1700s no longer exists. Over time, four successive churches were built. The fourth one, erected in 1895, still exists and has been beautifully restored. We were fortunate enough to meet a local man who had been involved in the restoration effort. He gave us an informal tour, pregnant with historical fact. Afterward, we found we could only see the gravesite from a distance because it was on private, wooded land. In exploring our distant past together, my father and I had a great time. I'll never forget it.

Later we drove to Washington, D.C. where we visited the Air and Space Museum. It was very interesting watching my father go from exhibit to exhibit. He pointed out planes like those he had flown. He showed me displays of historical persons he had known. Upon seeing an old black and white movie of three ancient biplanes doing aerobatics, he said he had known those planes personally. "I even helped to re-cover the wings on one of them," he told me.

Experiencing all of this with my father made me realize he had been an integral part of American aviation history. He had flown everything from ancient crates to the modern aircraft of his era. He had built planes for Lockheed, like Lockheed's Electra, similar to the one that Amelia Earhart flew when she was lost. As an A&E mechanic, he had repaired planes of all sorts. I believe this was the moment I realized I had to document his life as it paralleled and intertwined with aviation development.

Things kept radically changing in the world. In February 1991, the Warsaw Pact was dissolved and the Eastern European nations were no longer under the rule of the USSR. Then, unbelievably, the Soviet Union itself suddenly disintegrated in December of that same year. In its place were fifteen separate and independent republics. As quickly as it began, the Cold War was over.

In 1992, Bill Clinton was elected the 42nd President of the United States. When my father was born, Woodrow Wilson had just become the 28th President. President Wilson was the first of fifteen presidents who held office during my father's lifetime.

In 1993, my father underwent triple bypass heart surgery. I took time off work to be with him and drove him to the hospital prior to his operation. He checked in early in the morning and was in good spirits. My father was always very accepting of circumstances beyond his control. He was that time as well.

The operation took several hours and I stood by in the waiting room. When the surgery was completed, the surgeon came out and talked to me. He said a lot of calcification had broken loose during the procedure and gone to my father's brain. The doctor couldn't say what effect, if any, this would have on my father. He said the result is like having many little strokes. "We'll just have to wait and see what happens," he told me. My father had also had heart palpitations while on the operating table. I wasn't exactly sure what that meant, but it apparently caused momentary oxygen deprivation to his head.

Despite these unfortunate events, he did make it through surgery and was taken to the Intensive Care Unit (ICU). He was in ICU for two or three days. I visited him while he was there, but he was really out of it most of the time. It took him a very long time to regain full consciousness.

Upon discharge from ICU, my father was transferred to a nearby rehabilitation center. He spent two weeks there. I visited him as often as possible, doing what I could for him. Once I even shaved him. He complained to me that when he looked at the clock on the wall, it had a brown streak through it. The little strokes he had experienced during surgery had affected his eyesight. I also noticed an extreme change in my father's ability to think. It was as though I had taken one person to the hospital and brought a different person home.

After his release from the rehabilitation center, my father returned to his mobile home. Fortunately, Thelma's son and family lived very close by. They looked in on my father during the week and I drove up most weekends to do what I could for him.

Prior to his surgery, my father had cooked for himself, had taken computer classes and had been very active in a variety of organizations. He belonged to the Masonic Lodge, Scottish Rite, VFW, Hump Pilots Association, Eastern Star, Sons of

*Kenneth in front of a DC-3 at the National Air & Space Museum
(Washington, D.C., 1990)*

*Kenneth in front of the
first Round the World Flight
aircraft (National Air &
Space Museum, 1990)*

the American Revolution, and the Shriners. After his surgery though, he didn't cook or take classes or attend many of his organizations' activities. I guess it was too hard for him. I arranged for Meals on Wheels to deliver food to his home, but all he managed to do was sit in his recliner chair all day. I tried to get him to walk, but he had no interest in doing that either.

From the time of my father's surgery until 1995, I spent a great deal of my time driving back and forth between Santa Rosa and San Jose. I brought him down to my house whenever possible and did things for him in Santa Rosa when I stayed there. My father was taking the bus during this time because his doctor had reported his physical problems to the Department of Motor Vehicles, which, in turn, had taken away his driver's license. He signed over the title to his car to me and I used it to take him places. In 1994, I drove him to a Hump Pilot's Association meeting in Sacramento, California. I had to help him register and settle into his room—things he had been doing for himself before his operation, but now needed my help in doing.

Without my realizing it, my father's health was gradually deteriorating. The Meals on Wheels food was awful and he wasn't exercising. Eventually his doctor told him he would have to change his lifestyle immediately or he would be dead within six months. At that point, he called me and said, "Ken, I'm ready to move into a retirement home." I told him, "Okay, I'll take care of it."

Because my father was a Mason, I took him on a tour of the Masonic Retirement home in the San Francisco Bay area. It was a very large, impersonal place. In order to become a resident he would have had to turn over all of his assets to the home. That never became an issue though, because he didn't like the place at all. Soon after that, I checked out retirement facilities for active adults close to my home. I took my father around to what I thought were the top three, saving the one I thought best for last. Just as I suspected, he really liked the last place we visited—The Atrium.

He moved into The Atrium, 1009 Blossom River Way in San Jose, in 1995. To reduce his expenses, we put his mobile home up for sale. It took a year to sell, but we finally managed to sell it to the mobile home park's assistant manager and his wife. Now that my father was living closer to me, I could visit him much more often and take him places, like to Masonic Lodge meetings. He settled into his new home and seemed quite content. He was surrounded by people and eating well. Things were looking up for him.

In August 1997, I was shocked to find my second wife, Juliette, had filed for divorce. She was calling it quits after thirteen years of marriage. As my father had been with me, I guess I was a bit out of touch with the emotional realities of my marriage. While stumbling around in a mental fog at this turn of events, I moved in with my father at The Atrium. Due to the arbitrariness of life, a circle was completed. Where my father had looked out for me when I was very young before a distance came between us, I was now in a position to look out for him. At his time of greatest need, I suddenly had the time and the closeness to take care of my father.

Because he was diabetic, I gave him his shots when we were away visiting relatives in Southern California or out to an Air Show. I chauffeured him to his new doctors and I kept him company, which he seemed to enjoy very much. He even commented on how much I was taking care of him. I told him, "You took care of me when I was little, now it's my turn to take care of you." He accepted that and put me in charge of his life.

I tried to keep my father active and interested. I encouraged him to build a model airplane. He tried, but made a real mess of it. I took over the task, asking his opinion on everything I did, so that he was engaged. I took him to Air Shows and took pictures of airplanes from his era. I followed along with him during the 1997 reenactment of Amelia Earhart's world flight.

World Flight 1997 consisted of a 46-year-old Texas aviator and business woman named Linda Finch flying a restored Lockheed Electra 10E along a similar route as that taken by Amelia Earhart during her ill-fated 1937 journey. I took my father to Oakland Airport for Linda's departure and back again for her return at the completion of the flight. In between, I monitored the two Internet web sites dedicated to the flight, printing out the flight's progress and surrounding events and shared it with my father. He came to look forward to each day's reports as a real life serial.

We drove to Oakland Airport at the conclusion of World Flight where we met the Channel 7 News reporter Lyanne Melendez broadcasting the story. I introduced her to my father and gave her a brief background on his connection to the event. Unfortunately, when she attempted to interview him, he wasn't able to verbalize his Lockheed Electra experience. The major reason for this was his post-surgery condition, but also, my father was not a conversationalist. He wasn't shy, but he wasn't a braggart either.

At the same time I was taking my father out to Air Shows and following World Flight 1997, I was writing down his history. I went through his photographs and had him tell me about each one. He couldn't remember some things very well, but when it came to his early flying days, he could tell me the complete story behind each picture. I began writing down everything I learned in chronological order. After I wrote a section, I had my father read it for accuracy and expansion.

In 1997, The Atrium newsletter came out with an article about my father and me. The article was a concise history of my father and our situation together. I include an excerpt here for that reason and because it describes the environment I had set up for my father.

"Meet the Chastains"
(Written by AS – The Atrium Mirror, January – February 1997)

"Kenneth Chastain and Kenneth Jr. are unique in The Atrium. They are father and son residents. I wonder if any other residence has a similar combination in their residents?

Ken Sr. is a former transport and bomber pilot of the WWII era. He flew the "hump" in the China/Burma/India Theater, search and rescue in B-25s and was a flight instructor at Santa Maria in Stearman biplanes, as well. He flew the DC3s, DC4s and DC6s as a civilian pilot.

There are many mementos of his career visible in their apartment. There are some spectacular models of the various aircraft he has flown hanging from the ceiling. I observed another one under construction. It is a B-25, made famous by Jimmy Doolittle in his carrier-based raid on Tokyo early in WWII.

Ken and his son have a sizable collection of photos, certificates and clippings documenting his adventures and, dare I say, exploits. All this was marvelous for me to see, because I have always been an aviation fan. It was particularly interesting because a lot of these airplanes are now only to be seen in old photos and museums.

There are numerous mementos, some of which are quite imposing. In particular, a beautiful wooden propeller with a big clock mounted in the hub. There are lots of patches that went on flight jackets, medals and similar memorabilia. I saw, and we talked about, planes I had forgotten ever existed. I would have loved to spend more time with them, but it would have been an imposition on their hospitality.

He closed out his multiengine career flying for World Airways, based in Oakland, in the DC6. It was great fun, and a privilege for me, to have him and Ken Jr. share their times and experiences with me.

Ken Jr. is now the primary care giver. Ken Sr. moved here about a year and a half ago from his residence in Santa Rosa. Eyesight problems, compounded by the loss of his driver's license, made it imperative that he have some assistance. Ken Jr. managed to commute for a time, but it was far too demanding for him.

After looking [at] several places, Ken Sr. saw The Atrium and liked it best. He lived alone until about six months ago, when Ken Jr. moved in to increase his support for his dad. Not only is their situation unique—so are they . . . "

In October 1997, pop country singer John Denver died in a plane crash off of the California coast. I came home to find my father had cut an article about it from the newspaper. At first I was surprised at this. I didn't think he was a John Denver fan, but upon reflection, I realized he had done that very thing in his early years. When I was moving him I found a large cardboard box filled with newspaper articles with photographs from the Thirties and early Forties describing air crashes of the day—and there were lots of crashes back in the early days of aviation.

In January 1998, I was sent out of town on business. While I was away my father fell. Because The Atrium staff checked on residents who didn't come to dinner, he was soon discovered. The staff called an ambulance that took my father to the nearest hospital. First thing the next morning, I drove back to town and went to see him. He was still in emergency. They didn't check him in because it was a Kaiser Hospital and he wasn't on the Kaiser health plan. He had been stuck in the emergency room all night.

I got him into the car and took him back to The Atrium. Once there he settled into his favorite chair and seemed to be okay, but as the day wore on, his back began to bother him. He eventually went to bed and refused to get up to eat. He said he hurt too badly. Because he was a diabetic, it was necessary to get him to eat. When I realized he needed help I couldn't provide, I arranged for a non-emergency ambulance to take him to a convalescent home.

My father never recovered from his fall. After three days at the convalescent home he was transferred to a hospital where he stayed six weeks. After a minor surgery, he was released to another convalescent facility to build up his strength so he could return home. On March 9, 1998, at 7:05 A.M., my father passed away of congestive heart failure at the age of 84. On March 11, he was buried next to his third wife, Thelma, in Santa Rosa Memorial Park. The last years of my father's life had provided us the opportunity to come together in a way I never thought possible. The time we were close was short, but fulfilled my lifelong dream.

When I notified the HPA of my father's death, they listed his name in their newsletter (Spring 1998, page 16) along with other "Humpsters" who had passed away. The section of the newsletter where the deceased were listed was called "Last Formation"—a name quite apropos for flyers. It was also a good way to sum up my father's life as a flier and a patriot.

Lifetime flying buddies. Left to right: Forest Wiley and Kenneth at a Hump Pilot's Reunion (most likely taken in the very early 1990s)

Kenneth L. Chastain (1913–1998)